W9-CZB-515

THEOLOGIANS TODAY: HENRI DE LUBAC

Other titles in the THEOLOGIANS TODAY series:

Hans Urs von Balthasar
Yves M. J. Congar, OP
F. X. Durrwell, CSSR
Hans Küng
Karl Rahner, SJ
Edward Schillebeeckx, OP
F. J. Sheed

THEOLOGIANS TODAY: a series selected and edited by Martin Redfern

HENRI DE LUBAC, SJ

SHEED AND WARD · LONDON AND NEW YORK

First published 1972

Sheed & Ward Inc, 64 University Place, New York, N.Y. 10003
and Sheed & Ward Ltd, 33 Maiden Lane, London WC2E 7LA

Nihil obstat: John M. T. Barton, S.T.D., L.S.S., Censor
Imprimatur: ✠ Victor Guazzelli, V.G.
Westminster, 15 April, 1972

Library of Congress Catalog Number 72-2164

This book is set in 12/14 Monotype Imprint

Made and printed in Great Britain by
Billing & Sons Limited, Guildford and London

CONTENTS

Sources and Acknowledgments

"Christianity and History" and "The Sacraments as Instruments of Unity" (1947[4]) are from *Catholicism: A Study of Dogma in Relation to the Destiny of Mankind*, London, Burns & Oates and New York, Sheed & Ward, 1950.

"Ludwig Feuerbach, Protagonist of Atheist Humanism" (1945) is from *The Drama of Atheist Humanism*, London and New York, Sheed & Ward, 1949.

"The Family of God" (1953) is from *The Splendour of the Church*, London and New York, Sheed & Ward, 1956.

INTRODUCTION

The last twenty-five years, and in particular the last ten years, have seen a remarkable flowering of Roman Catholic theology. But for the non-specialist—for the busy parish priest, the active layman, the student—the very wealth of this development presents a range of problems. With which theologian does he begin? Which theologians will he find the most rewarding? Can he ignore any of them?

There are no quick or final answers to such questions, of course, but I hope that this new to find their own answers more easily. It is designed to achieve two main purposes: Each individual book provides a short but representative introduction to the thought of an outstanding Catholic theologian of the present day, and the series as a whole demonstrates the kind of relationship existing between the best contemporary Catholic theology and official Church teaching.

Both purposes are met by the framework common to all the books. For each book I have selected—and arranged in order of original publication—four pieces which indicate the range in time, approach, and special interest of the theologian concerned. Partly to make my selections more 'objective', but mainly to emphasise the close connection between the theologian's writing and the teaching of Vatican II, I have keyed the articles to the four major documents of that Council—the four Constitutions, on the Church, on Revelation, on the Liturgy, and on the Church in the Modern World.

The selections are very much my own. The theologians themselves, or other editors, would doubtless have made different choices. Nevertheless, I feel that—granted my self-imposed limitations of space and conciliar theme, and the further necessary limitations imposed by copyright or by a proper preference for the out-of-print or inaccessible over the widely available—I have done my own best for men to whom I owe a large debt of gratitude.

Both the pioneer nature and the wide range of Henri de Lubac's learning are well exemplified in this selection. The third article, on Feuerbach, is typical of his critical and yet wholly sympathetic interest in modern atheist and political thought—an interest which must surely have influenced the Constitution on the Church in the Modern World some twenty years later. Equally clear from the other articles is de Lubac's deep biblical and patristic scholarship, and his overriding pastoral concern.

MARTIN REDFERN

1. Christianity and History

"In carefully planning and preparing the salvation of the whole human race, the God of supreme love, by a special dispensation, chose for himself a people to whom he might entrust his promises. First he entered into a covenant with Abraham [cf. Gen 15:18] and, through Moses, with the people of Israel [cf. Ex 24:8]. To this people which he had acquired for himself, he so manifested himself through words and deeds as the one true and living God that Israel came to know by experience the ways of God with men."—*Dogmatic Constitution on Divine Revelation*, IV, 14.

I

Christianity brought something absolutely new into the world. Its concept of salvation is not merely novel in comparison with that of those religions in existence at the time of its birth. It is a unique phenomenon in the religious history of mankind.

For what, in fact, do we witness outside Christianity whenever a religious movement rises above the domain of sense and effectively transcends the limit of nationality? In every case, though appearances may differ considerably, the basis is the same—an individualist doctrine of escape. It was this that inspired ancient mysticism, whether it sought to escape the vicissitudes of the sub-lunary world or to pass over the outer circle of the cosmos and to penetrate into the realm of intelligible Essences or even beyond. The Greek sage, though in a different sense from the saint, was a being apart. His contemplation was solitary. Flight, Escape: that in fact was Plato's dictum regarding the soul that acknowledges in itself a principle superior to the world. Plotinus, in his turn, recommended to his disciple the "flight of the alone to the Alone", and then Porphyry expatiates on the setting free and the *withdrawal* of the soul. The same terms may be encountered in the religious philosophies of India. The adepts of ancient Brahmanism purposed to flee by way of the gates of the moon and the sun in order to be united with the unfathomable Prajâpati. Though the six classical *darsana* rejected these childish imaginings, nonetheless they preserved an idea of salvation formed on the same pattern, and there is no essential difference from this point of view between Sâmkhya philosophers who hold the enduring plurality of liberated souls as of so many impenetrable monads and the thinkers of the Advaita —that absolute *reductio ad absurdum* of the world— who seek to set themselves free from the illusion of the cosmos so as to be absorbed in the unity of the Supreme Being. With the Buddhist, too, it is the same act of negation, whether he denies the existence of the world or believes in the reality of his present wretchedness; and he who practises charity to a degree that sometimes reaches the sublime in the last resort reliquishes even that. Asanga, the great mystical doctor of the Mahâyâna, when he starts to map out the path of his bodhisattva's ascent from "world" to "world" until he reaches the very highest state, which is that of Nirvâna, as a matter of course describes it as a whole series of evasions: *niryàna*; so much so that it has been said that Buddhism's only God is Escape.

Every adept has his method. For some it is initiation into secret rites, for others asceticism and ecstasy, for a few philosophy. Some consider that definitive escape is open only to that small number of privileged souls who alone are recipients of a particle of the divine Essence, whereas the "Hylics", the "Abhavya", and the "Agotraka" are condemned to languish for ever in their prison. Others, less exclusive, readily believe that all men, indeed all living creatures, can attain salvation either in the course of their life or by means of a whole series—longer or shorter—of reincarnations. Sometimes the escape that is sought will consist in a total rejection, a radical negation, and sometimes it will be a higher understanding. Sometimes it will be hoped for in a perfect form and at others "as far as possible". Some of the saved separate themselves disdainfully from all that is profane, others will be moved by pity. The moral value of the different systems varies considerably. So does their spiritual depth; but in this connection the achievements of Greek thought, though it reached a very high level, cannot be compared with the heights of Indian thought. Sometimes understanding is imprisoned in myth, and sometimes it is turned inwards in pure reflection—or what seems to be. Yet running all through these many differences there is always agreement about the basis of the problem and its presuppositions: the world from which escape must be sought is meaningless, and the humanity that must be outstripped is without a history.

The "eternal return", from which nothing may be expected, in each of its phases—the Great Year,

Mahâkalpa, Jubilee or whatever it is called—the end of one being the beginning of another, with never a forward movement, how overpoweringly monotonous it all is! "There will be another Socrates, another everybody, with the same friends and the same fellow citizens; and all this will occur not once, but frequently, or rather, all things will be eternally restored", and also eternally broken and destroyed, for after the period of growth comes the period of decline and the continuing series of rebirths that are also one continual death: "death made immortal", says St Maximus. The sage, thus staving off his hunger for eternity, may well be deluded for a space by the thought that he is master of the world rhythm—the rhythm of *yin* and *yang*, Brahmâ breathing in and out, the dance of Siva making and destroying worlds, endless alternation of enmity and amity—or that he captures it all in the net of his aesthetic contemplation. Yet in its toils the human mass threshes about vainly in the same unchanging state of servitude.

II

Amid this universal chorus Christianity alone continues to assert transcendent destiny of man and the common destiny of mankind. The whole history of the world is a preparation for this destiny. From the first creation to the last end, through material opposition and the more serious opposition of created freedom, a divine plan is in operation, accomplishing its successive stages among which the Incarnation stands out as chief. So in close connection with the social character of dogma there is another character, equally essential, and that is the historic. For if the salvation offered by God is in fact the salvation of the human race, since this human race lives and develops in time, any accountof this salvation will naturally take a historical form—it will be the history of the penetration of humanity by Christ.

In the schemes we have set out above "the unfolding of time is a development without substance, in which nothing changes because everything changes". For Christianity, on the contrary, the course of history is indeed a reality. It is not mere barren dispersal but possesses, so to say, a certain ontological density and a fecundity. It is no longer, as in Platonism, merely "this moving image of unmoving eternity", "this eternal image without end" which is "unfolded in a circle following the law of numbers", this *aïdion*, a pale reflection of the *aiōnion*. Development no longer seems a circular series comprising generation and corruption connected together according to that principle by which the "fact that generation is ever renewed is the nearest approach to eternal being". *Circuitus illi jam explosi sunt*, says St Augustine: that is the triumphant cry of the Christian to whom God the Creator and Saviour has been revealed. The infernal cycle is disrupted. Facts are no longer phenomena, but events, acts. Forthwith something new is wrought—birth, real growth; the whole universe grows to maturity. Creation is not merely maintained, but is continuous. The world has a purpose and consequently a meaning, that is to say, both direction and significance. The entire human race, the child of God, sustained through all the disconcerting variety of its activities—*ab Abel justo usque ad novissimum electum*—by those two hands of God, the Word and the Holy Spirit, that despite its mistakes have never entirely loosened their hold, in this one great movement sets forth to the Father. The divine Will, controlling all things, brings it infallibly into port.

For there is a port, a definite terminus. The whole universe cries out for its delivery and it is sure to obtain it. Its groaning is begotten by hope. On that Christian tradition is unanimous, whatever the doctrinal differences—numerous and sometimes deep as they are—about the end of time or its beginnings, or even about the necessity for a temporal development of the human world at all. Such indeed is Origen's thought, in spite of a certain hesitation due rather to his overriding anxiety to preserve liberty of thought than to a too persistent Hellenism. He says: *In unum sane finem putamus quod bonitas Dei per Christum suum universam revocet creaturam.* Just as God rested on the seventh day after he had created the world, so the world, having completed its course, will rest in God. "Then time shall be no more" (Rev 10:6). All things shall be renewed: *caelum novum, nova terra.* The resurrection, which shall indicate the passing of time into eternity, will be a definitive transformation of the universe in the words of St Isidore, "a new earth will be created to contain the bodies that have been made new; that is to say, the whole nature of our earth will be transformed into a spiritual state, free, thenceforward, from any change."

Consequently, if Christians continue to proclaim louder than all others the need to flee from the world, *fugiendum a saeculo*, it is with quite a different meaning and with another emphasis. If they insist on the vanity of earthly and temporal things it is on account of those who consider these things only as they are in appearance, making them the objects of their love in themselves, whereas whatever is real about them is a summons to look beyond them. Time is vanity only for one who, using it unnaturally, desires to establish himself in it—and to think of nothing but a "future" is to establish oneself in time. Of necessity we must find a foothold in time if we are to rise into eternity; we must use time. The Word of God submitted himself to this essential law: he came to deliver us from time, but by means of time—*propter te factus est temporalis, ut tu fias aeternus* (St Augustine). That is the law of the Incarnation and it must undergo no Docetist mitigation. Following Christ's example, "loyally and with no cheating", every Christian must acquiesce in that state of engagement in time which gives him part and lot in all history, so that his connection with eternity is not unrelated to a past that he knows is immense and a future the length of which is hidden from him.

Before it was reflected in formulae and theories this belief found spontaneous expression through the selection of symbols and other usual representations. So it is that the old image of the ascent of the individual from sphere to sphere soon gives way to that of a collective progress from one age to another. We know the importance—real or symbolic—of cosmography in Hellenistic mysteries, in Pythagoreanism or neo-Platonism, and the place that the paths of the heavenly bodies, speculations about the planest and their approaches, the adornments of the soul, astral bodies and *media*, held in these systems. In India the mystic scheme is of a similar kind. The *bhûmika* of the Upanishad, the *bhûmi* of the Buddhist Mahâyâna are arranged in a series to be used as temporary mansions by the being that issues from the prison of our bodies. Each one of these dwellings is described with all its characteristics and many subtle distinctions.

In Gnosticism and later on in Manichaeism all this is to be found again, and in abundance. But authentic Christianity, though it did not at once give up all images of this sort, no longer attaches any importance to them. In Christian writers only traces of them continue to appear, and these are outside the stream of living thought. When they wish to symbolize the spiritual impulse their images are taken from Scripture rather than from the stars and the planets: Jacob's ladder, the gates of the city of God described by Ezekiel, the new Jerusalem of the Book of Revelation, the resting-places of the Jews in the desert. The resting-places to the number of forty-two were at first understood as the temporal sequence of the generations which led up to Christ, "the forty fathers according to the flesh by whom was brought about his descent to us", "as far as the Egypt that is this world"; even from such a figure, and one that was quite as obviously cosmographic as Jacob's ladder, teaching of a historical nature could be taken, by the method of analogy, thus revealing the mysteries of our Saviour's humanity. Irenaeus, for example, just like his gnostic adversaries, can believe in the reality of the seven heavens that make up this world, and he seems to rejoice at the idea that Moses must have been thinking of this when he ordered the making of the seven-branched candlestick; nor has he any doubt that Isaiah is alluding to it when he enumerates the "seven forms of worship". Origen, on the contrary, in his answer to Celsus, is careful to specify that "this is mentioned nowhere in scripture". But nonetheless both of them are in agreement on the essential point, and all who come after them concur in this. How should they have need of intermediaries whom the one Mediator brings directly to the Father? And what do they want with seven gates since Christ is the one gate through which they pass from Egypt to the Promised Land? Moreover, they have all understood the warning given by the angel after Christ had disappeared into the heavens. There is always more commentary on Pentecost than on the Ascension—Pentecost is still the more solemn festival—

and the Ascension itself is regarded in its relation to Pentecost according to Jesus' direction: *Expedit vobis ut ego vadam. . . . Si autem abiero, Spiritum mittam ad vos.* Contemplation of heaven will not distract the attention that must be given to the divine work which goes forward on earth, carried out with earthly materials but not for earthly purposes; a work that is accomplished in the Church wherein is prepared, and is already being realized in secret, the glory of him who humbled himself. And if the Master seems to have left his own for ever, yet we know that we must await, must hasten on, the time of his return: *unde missurus est Spiritum . . . unde venturus est. . . .*

III

Henceforward the stages of history are important, they are in reality stages of an essentially collective salvation. It is true, of course, that calculations of this sort have to be made, as Durandus of Mende remarks, *potius mystice quam chronice.* We must not expect too much precision. The system handed down by tradition was kept entire; only its subject-matter was changed. The number of stages—dispensations, laws, economies, testaments—was predetermined by the perfections, the "mysteries", to be found in certain numbers. Authors are not always in agreement as to their precise number, since the symbolic reasons or the circumstances that inspire their choice differ from one to another. But the differences are not contradictions and generally they are more apparent than real. Yet if one pressed details the complications would be extreme, for the Fathers' imagination found a great satisfaction in playing with combinations of numbers, whereby they exercised their ingenuity with subdivisions, additions and multiplications. We need only consider the principal systems, which, at first unrelated to one another, were afterwards harmonized by a differentiation between "times" and "ages". So we have on the one hand the system of four times, since four is a number that of its nature is universal—there are four elements, four seasons, four regions of the universe, the four pillars of the tabernacle, the four horses of Ezekiel's chariot, the four Gospels and the four rivers of Paradise. The four times may all be found in history or the fourth may be kept for the future life, according as the law received by Noah is added or not to the natural law, the law of Moses and the law of the Gospel. The first method of calculation was that used by St Irenaeus; the second, employed as early as St Gaudentius, prevailed from St Augustine onwards. On the other hand there is the system of the six ages or "centuries", which is extended to seven or sometimes even to eight, for these two last numbers are pre-eminently the perfect numbers and contain mysteries.

The combinations in this case are many, for each one represents some "mystic reason". Thus it is that the seventh age, which according to the most usually accepted notion is the age of eternity, beginning at the end of time, may come to mean the period of the final struggle against anti-Christ, or even be added to the sixth age, from the time of our Saviour's Incarnation. As for the eighth age, which bears to the seven others the same relation as the Gospel does to the Law or as Sunday does to the Sabbath, it is the age of *Christus Oriens*, of the resurrection, and therefore of that full and final blessedness which follows the rest of the seventh day: *in octavo, resurrectionis est plenitudo*, as St Ambrose puts it. But these extensions apart, the division of human history into six ages, a practice of long standing in Judaism, was everywhere adopted in the Church. Does not the Bible teach that the world was created in six days? For each of these biblical days there is a corresponding age of the world. To each act of intervention required for the creation of the world there is the corresponding act which is necessary to lead it towards its end. The same number of ages go to its "perfecting" as there were days in its creation, Six days to make ready the mansion wherein Adam should reign, six ages to gather up this Adam again from the four quarters of the globe where he was scattered. This comparison, which the Fathers found useful in manifesting the truth of a single God who is both Creator and Saviour, shows just as clearly the corresponding truth about the world: nothing of the divine work shall be lost. The work of the Son completes and restores the work of the Father; the gifts of the Holy Spirit consecrate it. Whatever its weakness and its present state of wretchedness, this world is good and it will be saved.

It will be clearly seen that in this case there is no question of simple and more or less superficial theories. The contradiction that thus becomes manifest between Christianity and pagan thought is not just a difference between two sets of writers: it goes to the very foundation of religion. It is built into the doctrinal framework and finds eloquent expression in liturgical compositions. Of course there was no need for the Church to repudiate the harmony between the earth and the cosmos. Just as her doctors have preserved, often felicitously, many habits of thought and turns of phrase which are tainted in origin, so does the Church gather to its vast treasury riches rescued from all sides. It took the sumptuous setting of its worship from dying paganism, making a halo for the Sun of Justice out of the glory of the *Sol Invictus*, adoring its cathedrals with the signs of the zodiac, harmonizing its ceremonies with the rhythm of the seasons. But it is neither the natural cycle nor some extra-cosmic deliverance that is portrayed by the Church's liturgical year: it is the vast history of our redemption.

Compare it on this point, for example, with worship like that of the Mithraic mysteries. Within the Mithraeum everything, though under the sign of the twelve regions of heaven and the four elements, was at the same time under the sign of the seven planets: furniture and ornament included seven altars, seven knives, seven Phrygian caps, seven trees; among the statues, seven busts of the Gods. Origen mentions the scale of seven portals that was shown to the initiate, and nowadays there may be seen at Ostia the seven-arched portals outlined on the pavement of a Mithraeum; on the banks of the Rhine, whither soldiers of the Roman empire had transported their cherished worship, miniature scales have been found in many tombs. They were symbols of the seven degrees of Mithraic initiation by which the heavenly ascent of the worshipper was effected. Now in Christian liturgy there is one privileged part of the year which is also under the sign of the number seven. It is the season, with its imaginative rather than real divisions, which, beginning on Septuagesima, terminates on the Saturday *in Albis* or on Laetare Sunday, according as it is counted on the basis of seven times ten days or seven consecutive Sundays. But the symbolism of this series of seven is quite different. In the Babylonian captivity we have a figure of the long captivity of the whole human race from the time of its original sin down to its being set free by Christ, and in the forty years from the time of the exodus from Egypt to the entry into the promised land is figured its long earthly pilgrimage, the long ascent to its heavenly home. In practice, then, it is the whole of human history. We have here our six ages of the world, the six great stages of the redemption, with the addition of the final age which begins with the resurrection, the definitive sabbath, when Christ at last takes his rest, the seventh day which shall know no decline. The Scripture read in the breviary at the beginning of this period is the account of the creation, and the Gospel of the Mass is the parable of the labourers sent into the vineyard in whom tradition sees a figure of the divine economy; this also is the burden of the homily by St Gregory the Great read at Matins on that day. It is the history of salvation wrought by Christ, a single history with its components closely bound up together, wherein all the characters, labourers at an identical task, are mysteriously united, and where "escape" has no place.

IV

This conception of the history of the world, like the social conception of salvation with which it is allied, has its roots in Judaism. Yahweh is the living God, the God who speaks to man's heart, but also the God of history. The Jews believe that their people was created by him on Sinai and was scattered by him at the overthrow of Jerusalem; on the first occasion his instrument was Moses, on the second Nebuchadnezzar. Since it is he who made the past, he will rule the future and the destiny of his people is in his hands. As this little people came more in touch with its powerful neighbours and its intellectual bounds were widened, its faith also increased; and just as in the second part of the book of Isaiah universalism reaches its zenith, so, a little later, there appears in the book of Daniel a philosophy of universal history.

Before this Jeremiah had glimpsed that Judah of the prophets could not grow to maturity unless it were first uprooted, and since in his time the nation had no desire for reform he left it to rush to its downfall. He thought only of preparing for the nation to come which should rise from the ruin. Later, Ezekiel, able at that distance to view history in truer perspective, saw two periods in the development of God's kingdom; beyond the restoration of the nation, the first of Yahweh's victories over the world, he envisaged a definitive triumph. From the book of Daniel onwards this triumph appears as the end of human history, and it is allied with the physical transformation of the universe. Under the guise of four beasts—a lioness with eagle's wings, a bear, a leopard, and a horned beast terrible and wonderful—Daniel beheld four kingdoms which were symbols of the four empires, each one succeeded and absorbed by that which followed it, and together making up the empire of evil. This will be overcome by the empire of God wherein all the righteous, after their resurrection, shall have their part, all "the people of the saints of the most High whose kingdom is an everlasting kingdom".

Thus the idea of a divine work that the whole movement of the world should bring to fruition, the idea of the progress of mankind in its entirety towards a determined end, finds vigorous expression in the Hebrew world. There has been some attempt to belittle the originality of this idea. René Berthelot wrote in this connection:

In the eschatological and already apocalyptic predictions that terminate the prophetic literature, the end of the world entails its re-beginning, with the return of the blessings of Eden, the garden of God. This, it should be noticed, is a result of that very conception of a moral and social cycle, linked with the great astronomical and biological cycles and with the "Great Years" in the life of the world, found in Chaldea as in China; but in Jewish apocalyptic literature the cycle comes to an end when it has reached, once and for all, its original starting-place.

The clarity of this last remark excuses our dwelling on some other differences. A more serious objection to the originality of Israel comes from an examination of Mazdaism; at first sight it seems to bear a resemblance to Judaism that is all the more striking in that the history of religions can show no other such example.

According to the Gâthâs the world is proceeding to its end, and this end of the world is the "great event". Then when all things shall be revealed, man shall be judged by fire, which "will hurt the unrighteous and benefit the righteous". The faithful do not merely await this day of the "last crisis", they hasten on its advent and "make the world go forward" by their piety. By virtue of this they receive the title of benefactors, *saosyant*, a word which is not at all a proper name but a common title, just as Messiah was for long with the Jews. They show the most intense interest in "the greatest event of all" in which they will take part—obviously through their resurrection. And then upon the earth, reacts in the fire, the theocracy proclaimed by the Mazdean priests will become accomplished fact.

In the remainder of the Avesta, and in the Pahlavi books, the part played by God (Ahura Mazda) at the end of the world, and part the of the faithful in its completion, will appear of lesser importance in comparison with the work accomplished by the principal Saosyant and his assistants. The whole of history simply is divided into four periods of 3,000 years each. The first period is that of a purely spiritual creation. During the second the material world is formed (myths of the primordial Man and the primordial Bull). The third starts with the beginnings of the human race and is filled with the struggle between Ahura Mazda, "the very wise Lord", and Aura Mainyu, the "Adversary". Lastly Zoroaster appears, and that is the fourth period; each of its thousand year divisions begins under one of the three sons of the prophet, born in their time from his seed which has been preserved miraculously in sacred milk. Right at the end comes the time of the supreme Saosyant; surrounded by his six assistants he "will make the power of evil disappear", "will complete the world" and "will raise up bodies".

The similarity with Jewish Messianism is evident, though it will have been noticed that Mazdaism is inclined to a greater optimism, a more activist conception of the world's growing to maturity, which is the work of each individual. But it does not seem right, fundamentally, to explain the similarity by the influence of one on the other.

Some of the details of the Pahlavi apocalypse, particularly the prominence of the figure of the Saosyant, could have come from the Bible, but everything seems to point to the Gâthâs being anterior to the meeting of Jews and Persians in Babylon; on the other hand, if the breadth of view of the book of Daniel and its imaginative expression betray some contact with Persia, it is nonetheless the result of an entirely Jewish line of thought. In reality we have to do with two lines of thought, the convergence of which careful examination will reveal to be more apparent than real.

V

In ancient Persia, as among many of the Indo-European peoples, there was a myth concerning the conflagration of the world. It was a nature-myth and does not seem to have involved at first any religious or moral significance. It was incorporated by the Zoroastrian reform, provided with a chronology and with a superimposed last judgement, and came finally to be the whole end of the evolution of the world and the human race. Memories or legends of the national epic were afterwards interpreted in this sense, and the primitive myth was gradually invested with certain notions of a supposedly historical nature. But the eschatology still remained entirely of "scientific" inspiration. With Israel the opposite occurred.

Man and his destiny form the whole subject of the Bible; it is a drama, so to say, with two characters: Israel and Yahweh. Relations between them do not derive simply from the nature of things. Yahweh is not, like the other national Gods, physically bound to his people. If he is not served by them as he should be, in justice, not merely will he chastise them but he will abandon them for ever and raise up their destroyers. A historical fact lies at the origin of Israel, their choosing by Yahweh, followed by an alliance, a compact, *berit.* Israel is the people secured for himself by Yahweh. That is the concrete basis of the Decalogue: "I am the Lord thy God, who brought thee out of the land of Egypt, out of the house of bondage. Thou shalt not have strange Gods before me." Likewise the starting-point of Jewish eschatology is faith in Yahweh and his promises. It is the expectation of that day whereon all his power and faithfulness shall be made manifest. It is not the anticipation of some "natural" phenomena, but the hope—or fear—of an occurrence that will still be part of history, of a final judgement whereof past events are, so to say, an earnest.

In general the prophets spoke of God's action in history rather than of his action in nature. They lay greater stress upon Yahweh's part on the formation and leading of Israel than upon his making and governance of the world. After their threats against the unfaithful people they foretell the fall of the enemies of the holy people. The central purpose of their visions is not a cataclysm but the fall of empires

—even though their faith finds expression in images borrowed freely from nature and from fragments of mythology. With Ezekiel and the second Isaiah cosmic disturbances come to play an important part in the prophecies, though they appear as mere repercussions of human events, and if they are to be the concomitants of the last day and so prepare for the judgment they give no indication of when it will be. "No one knows the day or the hour. . . . The Son of man will come like a thief." However, when Israel, broadening its outlook, incorporated world history into its system, it took over also certain "scientific" ideas from its surroundings, so that the "Lord's day", as the Second Epistle of Peter bears witness, came to coincide in the end, though without losing its essential character, with world conflagration.

Mazdean eschatology is founded originally, then, on the myth of world conflagration, whereas the hope of Israel has its roots in history. This difference involves others which betoken it. In Mazdaism, although its calculations are small indeed as compared with Indian flights of fancy or indeed with the span of historic time, the end of the universe is primarily something afar off and, as it were, abstract; a belief without living connection with actual existence. In Israel, on the contrary, and from the very beginning, national history was a divine drama leading up to its final act on the day of Yahweh. Of its very nature Mazdaism—and this second remark is no less important—insists in the first place on an individual judgement and salvation, whereas it is only at a very late period that Jewish theology took any interest in the individual. To sum up: the last ordeal according to Mazdaism remains a drama that is essentially physical, arising from the fundamental structure of the cosmos; but the Gospel, in which Jewish thought is fulfilled, deals with a strictly moral drama in which man is an intensely interested actor, and in which he has a keen realization of being personally involved.

Thus it is not surprising that the "historicity" of Mazdaism has borne such fruit. It has not succeeded in grafting upon the human conscience the ideal that it perceived in the Gâthâs and in its relatively pure state was never a popular cult. Its earthbound prophesying, entirely lacking in mysticism, founders in a medley of undeveloped myth and artificial constructions which by their over-regular arrangement betray an outworn vein. To be sure it is not without interest to note that this religion, which has been described as the least pagan in the whole pagan world, should be the only one to show any resemblance, in such an important particular, with revealed religion. Yet what a gulf there is between the two! For Israel, history is the work of God in a sense that Mazdaism with its unresolved tendency to dualism could never achieve: "The Lord has done all this: he has prepared it from afar." "I made the earth and the men and the beasts that are upon the face of the earth, by my great power and by my stretched out arm: and I gave it to whom it seemed good in my eyes." So it is that the messianic hope of the Chosen People is not only proof against all disappointment, overcomes all obstacles: but rather engulfs them and draws from their substance the food of its irresistible strength and spreading scope.

One thing is certain, whatever the precise method or moment of its coming. This hope is so consubstantial with Jewish thought that, far from declining in the face of the discoveries that follow the growth of civilization or growing feeble as a result of its maturity, it contrives to incorporate everything—universalist views, cosmic speculations, progress in the spiritual life or attempts to form a system of humanist knowledge. It endows everything with an historical form, it makes of everything the work of its God and the instrument of his plans, growing ever more eager in expectation of an event that is at the same time ever nearer and ever more awe-inspiring. "With a single glance, at one leap, at one stroke, heaven is joined to earth and they are ineffably bound together" (G. Cattanui). The Bible makes an extraordinary impression on the historian: the contrast between the humble beginnings of Israel and the potency of the seed, or rather the explosives, which it contains; its concrete shape shrouded from the outset in the loftiest beliefs; then its stately expansion, its confident though hidden progress to a boundless and unpredictable end: nowhere else can be found anything in the least like it. Nothing resembles the stupendous incoherence of its prophetic literature; only a transfiguration of the whole, glimpsed in sudden flashes, can prevent overwhelming and endless contradictions. The historical character of the religion of Israel can be understood in all its originality only through its consummation in the religion of Christ. We should never forget that the explanation of Judaism is not to be found within itself.

2. The Sacraments as Instruments of Unity

"It is through the liturgy, especially the divine eucharistic sacrifice, that 'the work or our redemption is exercised'. . . The liturgy reveals the Church as a sign raised above the nations [cf. Is 11:12]. Under this sign the scattered sons of God are being gathered into one [cf. Jn 11:52] until there is one fold and one shepherd [cf. Jn 10:16]."—*Constitution on the Sacred Liturgy*, Introduction, 2.

Since the sacraments are the means of salvation they should be understood as instruments of unity. As they make real, renew or strengthen man's union with Christ, by that very fact they make real, renew or strengthen his union with the Christian community. And this second aspect of the sacraments, the social aspect, is so intimately bound up with the first that it can often be said, indeed in certain cases it must be said, that it is through his union with the community that the Christian is united to Christ.

That is the constant teaching of the Church, though it must be confessed that in practice it is too little known. Just as redemption and revelation, even though they reach every individual soul, are nonetheless fundamentally not individual but social, so grace which is produced and maintained by the sacraments does not set up a purely individual relationship between the soul and God or Christ; rather does each individual receive such grace in proportion as he is joined, socially, to that one body whence flows this saving life-stream. Thus it has been said that the causality of the sacraments is to be found not so much "in a paradoxical efficacy, in the supernatural order, of a rite or perceptible action, as in the existence of a society, which under the appearances of a human institution hides a divine reality" (Scheeben). All the sacraments are essentially sacraments of the Church; only in the Church do they produce their full effect, for only in the Church, "the society of the Spirit", is there, normally speaking, participation in the gift of the Spirit.

The first effect of Baptism, for example, is none other than this incorporation in the visible Church. To be baptized is to enter the Church. And this is essentially a social event, even in the primary, extrinsic meaning of the word. But its consequences are not solely juridical; they are also spiritual, mystical, because the Church is not a purely human society: whence comes the "character" conferred by Baptism, and, when the other requisite conditions are present, the sacramental grace of regeneration. So it is that by being received into a religious society one who has been baptized is incorporated in the Mystical Body: such is the twofold indivisible meaning of traditional expressions like *Ecclesiae Dei sociari*, *Ecclesiae incorporari*, *in corpus Ecclesiae transire*, and it is by this incorporation that each one receives the adoption of sons and is given life by the Holy Spirit. The first act is social a one.

Nor is the final consequence any less social in nature, though its meaning is in this case an entirely inward one. For if the sacraments derive their efficacy from the Church, it is still in view of the

Church that this efficacy is bestowed upon them. The water and blood which flowed from the side of Jesus on the Cross, the water of Baptism, the blood of the Eucharist, first fruits of the mystical union between Christ and his Church, are, at the same time, the streams at which that Church is nourished. As the water flows over our foreheads it does not merely effect a series of incorporations, but there takes place at the same time a "concorporation" of the whole Church in one mysterious unity. Baptismal regeneration, on a final analysis, is not confined in effect to one soul alone. "For in one Spirit", says the Apostle, "we were all baptized into one body." That is what St Irenaeus was at pains to make clear about both Baptism and Confirmation, working out a symbolism that has become less familiar to us nowadays, though it was for long a commonplace in sermons:

> The Holy Spirit came down on the Apostles that all nations might enter on the Life. And so they are gathered together to sing a hymn to God in all tongues. In this way the Holy Spirit brought the scattered peoples back to unity, and offered to the Father the first fruits of all nations. Indeed, just as without water no dough, not a single loaf, can be made of dry flour, so we who are many cannot become one in Christ without that water that comes from heaven. That is why our bodies receive by Baptism that unity which leads to life incorruptible, and our souls receive the same unity through the Holy Spirit.

Primitive inscriptions in Rome also furnish a commentary on this:

> Unto heaven is born a people of divine strain, begotten by the Holy Spirit who makes the waters fruitful.
>
> Amidst the waves Mother Church brings forth her unspotted offspring conceived by virtue of the Holy Spirit.
>
> Among those reborn is no difference: they are one through one immersion, one Spirit and one faith.
>
> And you who were begotten in these waters, come then to unity as you are called by the Holy Spirit that he may bestow his gifts upon you.

The language used by Ivo of Chartres is more significant still, forging as it does another link in the long chain of tradition. In dealing with the sacrifice of the new law in which the Church offers itself at the same time as it offers Christ, he portrays it made ready by previous rites to carry out this high office: *per aquam baptismatis adjuncta, chrismatis oleo peruncta, sancti Spiritus igne solidata, per humilitatis Spiritum hostia placens effecta*, so that through each one of us this one Church ever appears as the chief object as well as the chief minister of all the sacraments. *Sacramenta faciunt ecclesiam.*

The efficacy of Penance is explained like that of Baptism, for the relationship is quite as clear, in the case of the former, between sacramental forgiveness and the social reintegration of the sinner. The double functions of this sacrament as a disciplinary institution and as a means of inner purification are not merely associated in fact; they are united, if one may so put it, by the nature of things. The Church's primitive discipline portrayed this relationship in a more striking manner. The whole apparatus of public penance and pardon made it clear that the reconciliation of the sinner is in the first place a reconciliation with the Church, this latter constituting an efficacious sign of reconciliation with God. At the end of his *Quis dives salvetur* Clement of Alexandria relates the touching (perhaps legendary) story of the pagan who was converted by St John and afterwards fell away. By his patience, tears and prayers the Apostle managed to convert him again, that is to say, he "restored him to the Church". In St Cyprian's view, for instance, the priest's intervention has for its immediate effect this "return" of the sinner, this return of one who has been "cut off" (excommunicated) to the assembly of the faithful; the cleansing of the soul is a natural consequence of this reimmersion in the stream of grace, and it should be defined as a return to the "communion" of saints. It is precisely because there can be no return to the grace of God without a return to the communion of the Church that the intervention of a minister of that Church is normally required. "Only the whole Christ", said Isaac de Stella in the twelfth century, "the head upon his Body, Christ with the Church, can remit sins."

The sacrament in the highest sense of the word—*sacramentum sacramentorum, quasi consummatio spiritualis vitae et omnium sacramentorum finis*—the sacrament "which contains the whole mystery of our salvation", the Eucharist, is also especially the sacrament of unity: *sacramentum unitatis ecclesiasticae*.

Doubtless no Catholic, however ill-instructed in his religion, is ignorant of this. But is this capital truth understood in all its implications? When a thought is given to it, don't we often tell ourselves that this is only a secondary and additional consideration without which the doctrine of the Eucharist would still be complete? That at least is what the abundant literature on the subject would lead one to believe. In 1912 Dom J. Simon was able to report that contemporary authors did not seem to have attached great importance to this unitive force of the Eucharist, and to go on to remark that if *l'Année Liturgique* and a few rare works on mysticism had not been at pains to revive it, it would have been by that time a forgotten doctrine. Since then, in spite of many efforts, the situation seems much the same as far as the generality of Christians is concerned. Yet St Paul said: "For we being many are one bread, one body, all that partake of one bread"; and St Ignatius of Antioch: "There is but one chalice that you may be united in the blood of Christ." The Council of Trent teaches:

> It was the will of Christ to make of this sacrament the symbol of that Body of which he is himself the

> Head, to which he would bind us as his members by the close bonds of faith, hope and charity, so that all should be but one reality, with never a division.

It calls on "all those who bear the name of Christian" to come together "in this sign of unity, this bond of charity, this symbol of harmony". In his Apostolic Constitution of 1902 on the Eucharist Leo XIII defined it again as the *radix atque principium catholicae unitatis*.

Such teaching was not only general with the Fathers of the Church, it was in the very forefront of their thought. The choice among so many equally clear and beautiful texts is an embarrassing one. It must be enough to quote a few among many of them.

This, for example, is what St Cyprian says:

> How strong is Christian unanimity . . . , the sacrifice of the Lord itself proclaims it. For when the Lord calls his body the bread which is made up of many grains joined together, he means by that the union of all Christian people, which he contained within himself. And when he calls his blood the wine which is made into one drink of many grapes, he again means that the flock which we form is made up of individuals who have regained their unity.

And St John Chrysostom says:

> Let us learn the wonders of this sacrament, the

> purpose of its institution, the effects that it produces. We become one body, says the Scripture, members of his flesh, bones of his bones. That is what the food that he gives us effects: he joins himself to us that we may become one whole, like a body joined to its head.

The mysticism of St Cyril of Alexandria is especially insistent:

> To merge us in unity with God and among ourselves, although we have each a distinct personality, the only Son devised a wonderful means: through one only body, his own, he sanctifies his faithful in mystic communion, making them one body with him and among themselves. Within Christ no division can arise. All united to the single Christ through his own body, all receiving him, the one and indivisible, into our own bodies, we are the members of this one body and he is thus, for us, the bond of unity.
>
> We are all of us, by nature, separately confined in our own individualities, but in another way, all of us are united together. Divided as it were into distinct personalities by which one is Peter or John or Thomas or Matthew, we are, so to say, moulded into one sole body in Christ, feeding on one flesh alone. One Spirit singles us out for unity, and as Christ is one and indivisible we are all no more but one in him. So did he say to his heavenly Father, "That they may be one, as we are one".

And here is St Augustine speaking to the newly baptized in that direct style of the best of his homilies, in which poetry breaks through the homely dialogue:

> "The Body of Christ," you are told, and you answer "Amen." Be members then of the Body of Christ that your Amen may be true. Why is this mystery accomplished with bread? We shall say nothing of our own about it, rather let us hear the Apostle, who speaking of this sacrament says: "We being many are one body, one bread." Understand and rejoice. Unity, devotion, charity! One bread: and what is this one bread? One body made up of many. Consider that the bread is not made of one grain alone, but of many. During the time of exorcism, you were, so to say, in the mill. At baptism you were wetted with water. Then the Holy Spirit came into you like the fire which bakes the dough. Be then what you see and receive what you are.
>
> Now for the Chalice, may brethren, remember how wine is made. Many grapes hand on the bunch, but the liquid which runs out of them mingles together in unity. So has the Lord willed that we should belong to him and he has consecrated on his altar the mystery of our peace and our unity.

Lastly, St John Damascene, in whom the whole Greek tradition may be heard:

> If the sacrament is a union with Christ and at the same time a union of all, one with another, it

must give us real unity with those who receive it as we do.

In the train of the Fathers, who themselves merely commented on the scriptural and liturgical texts, the whole Latin Middle Ages were nourished on this teaching. Theologians, preachers, exegetes, liturgists, controversialists and poets reveal it one after another. To all it appears so fundamental that their discussions take it for granted. If it is not a speciality of learned speculation, no more is it the special preserve of any one school. The followers of Paschasius Radbertus, Rhabanus Maurus, or Ratramnus, as well as those of Florus or Amalarius, those who hold the theory of "Ambrosian metabolism", "Augustinian dynamism" or just Roman realism; whatever the exact relationship that they work out between "the body born of a virgin" and the eucharistic body; whether in their assertion of the sacramental presence they place the emphasis on the *mysterium* or the *veritas*; all are agreed in this: the result of the sacrament is unity. *In (hoc) sacramento fideles communicantes pactum societatis et pacis ineunt.* Thus is it worthy of the name of communion which is given to it. And that is why, even though the bread and wine are validly consecrated by schismatics, it can be said that there is a true Eucharist only where there is unity—*non conficitur ibi Christus, ubi non conficitur universus.* Like Scripture the Eucharist has a spiritual meaning; that is what is meant by the fraction, that action through which the disciples of Emmaus knew

Christ, an action that unlocks the mystery for us that we may discover there signified the Body of Christ which is the Church.

The symbolism of the elements gives rise to all sorts of developments, but there is no purpose in detailing them here. We merely quote, as typically representative of an explanation which goes back even in its details to the patristic age, the *de Sacramentis* of Master Simon (middle twelfth century):

> Why is Christ received under the form of bread and wine? It may be said that in the sacrament of the altar there are two things: the true body of Christ and what it signifies, namely, his mystical body which is the Church. Now as one loaf is made of many grains which are first wetted, then milled and baked to become bread, so the mystical body of Christ, that is to say the Church, formed by the gathering together of a multitude of persons, like to many grains, is wetted in the water of Baptism. It is then crushed between the two millstones of the old and New Testament or of hope and fear . . . , and in the last place it is baked in the fire of passion and sorrow that it may be made worthy to be the body of Christ. In truth the blessed martyr Ignatius wished to be united with this body in fullest reality when he said: "I am the wheat of Christ; let me be crushed by the teeth of the beasts to become the bread of Christ." Likewise wine is the product of many grapes; when they have been trodden and pressed

> in the wine press the must is left as worthless and the wine is stored; Holy Church, too, suffers by being beset in the world as in a wine press . . . where, as the wine is separated from the must, the wicked are cast away and the righteous put to the test. Rightly, then, such elements designate Christ's body, that is, the Church.

This same teaching emerges, clearly and continually, from a wealth of detail: the outward signs of the mystery, the bread and wine, proclaim *quod fideles in hoc sacramento in unam dilectionem convenire debent*. In this connection will be noted the important part played by suffering. It is the very crucible wherein unity is forged. That man who will not remain isolated must pass through it. For is not the Eucharist the memorial of the Passion? It was quite natural that the ears of wheat from which the bread of the offertory is made should be compared with that other ear of which our Saviour said that if it fell to earth and died it would increase a hundredfold. And does not the wonderful fruitfulness of that Divine Grain that lay for three days in the earth, lie in a multiplication which is for ever returning to unity? There is a poem ascribed to Hildebertus of Tours:

> Ex uno multis affluit copia grains,
> De quibus efficitur nunc unus in aethere panis:
> Nam quoties, Christo crescente, fide generamur,
> Ex uno grano quasi plurima grana creamur,

Cujus dum sapimus carnes, et sanguinis haustum,
Unus fit panis, vinumque fit hoc holocaustum. . . .

From the eleventh century onwards these doctrines were systematized in a theory which is structurally Augustinian. At that time a distinction began to be made between three elements as it were in the sacrament, three stages of depth, all three of them essential to its integrity: the *sacramentum tantum*, that is to say the outward sign; the *sacramentum et res*, what is contained under the sign, the sign in its turn of a deeper reality; and the *res tantum*, the definitive fruit of the sacrament. The first of these three elements was constituted, together with the sacrificial rite, by the species of bread and wine: *forma panis et vini*; the second by the body of Christ itself: *veritas carnis et sanguinis*; and the third by the unity of the Church: *virtus unitatis et caritatis*. And just as the body of Christ was signified more exactly by the bread and his blood by the wine, so the Church, which is also the body of Christ, seemed signified by the consecrated bread, whilst the wine changed into the blood of Christ was naturally the symbol of love which is like the blood wherein is the life of this great body. Such is the doctrine which, outlined by Fulbert of Chartres and Guitmond of Aversa, and developed at the beginning of the twelfth century by Alger of Liège, is to be found in its precise and final shape in most of the *Libri Sententiarum*. From that time onwards it ranks as a classical doctrine. It may be found in Otto of Lucca and Peter Lombard as in Hugh of St Victor or in Baldwin of Canterbury, in Abelard's disciples as in the *Sententiae Florianenses* or the *Sententiae Parisienses*. The great Scholastics took it up; St Thomas Aquinas drew on it more than once. At the beginning of the thirteenth century Innocent III, after setting it out at length in his great work on the mystery of the altar, crystallized it in a letter the very terms of which we have just been using. Durandus of Mende reproduces it in his well-known *Rationale*; in it he copies Innocent's phrases word by word. In the following centuries the same doctrine is still current, and the Council of Trent reproduces it in all its essentials.

O signum unitatis! O vinculum caritatis! Gradually the doctrine was forgotten; this cannot be accounted for simply by the fact that the framework of sacramental theory had been modified, for the doctrine was independent of this framework and to some extent was responsible for it. Nor, save in a secondary sense, can insistence on the reality of the eucharistic presence be made the chief culprit for this loss; Berengarius's principal opponents were extremely careful to guard against such insistence being interpreted in any way as a repudiation of other aspects of the mystery. All the same a change was gradually wrought in men s habits of mind. Their whole picture of the world was changed. Just as they would no longer see the spiritual reflected in the sensible or the universal and particular as reciprocally symbolical, so the universal and particular as reciprocally symbolic, so the idea of the relationship between the physical body of Christ and his Mystical Body came to be forgotten. It was like the slow atrophy of an unused sense. Faith, though remaining orthodox, was straitened, because it was no longer nourished by "intelligence". There are doubtless not a few in our day inclined to think that there is but a vague extrinsic analogy between these two meanings of the "body". That was certainly not the opinion of our forebears, whether, in the first of the two uses of the term, they were concerned with the fleshly body of Christ as it was during his earthly life and on Calvary, or whether they envisaged this body in its risen, its "spiritual", state. When, with St Augustine, they heard Christ say to them: "I am your food, but instead of my being changed into you, it is you who shall be transformed into me," they unhesitatingly understood that by their reception of the Eucharist they would be incorporated the more in the Church. They could see a profound identity between the mysteries of the "real presence" and of the "mystical body". And this identity was taken for granted in all their—frequently lively—discussions on the question of the *corpus triforme* or the *triplex modus corporis Christi*. It is here that may be found the explanation of the fact that, in the words of some of them, the first of these two mysteries, the real presence, stands out less boldly, and also the reason for the changes in their terminology whereby the two attributes *mysticum* and *verum* come to be transposed without any essential change in doctrine.

"Jesus Christ bears us in himself; we are, if I may

dare to say so, more truly his than his own body." That is an astounding sentence of Bossuet's, though he is careful to qualify it with "whoever has the spirit of charity and Christian unity will understand what I mean". And he goes on. "What he does in his divine body is a true pattern of what should be accomplished in us." Bossuet owes this fundamental principle, together with his daring manner of speech, to his constant study of the Fathers. "Everything in Christ," St Augustine tells us, for example, "his life, his death and his resurrection, his actions, his body even, are symbolic of Christian life, the 'sacrament' of that spiritual man who is also one and universal." Before him Origen had brought out with greater precision the relation of symbolic efficacy between the individual body of Christ, *sōma tupikon*, and his "real" Body which is the Church, *ekklēsia sōma*. He came to the conclusion that the final result, the "truth" of sacramental communion, was union with the Church within whose heart the Word resounds, for it is indeed the real presence of the Logos. During the Middle Ages the essentials of his thought are to be found on all sides. So William of St Thierry, though like many others he distinguishes, but with additional slight differences of his own, a threefold body of Christ, goes on at once to say that in truth this body is one though there are three ways in which it may be considered by faith and adhered to by piety; so that from that body which was hung on the tree to the Church itself "there is unceasing continuity".

We have just come to the fringe of a problem, or rather a whole series of problems, which cannot be examined more deeply here. It must suffice that they have thus been brought to the notice of theologians. Yet in whatever light we look on the efforts at system-making shown by the history of theology, the basic idea that these efforts sought to emphasize cannot be considered a more or less wild speculation or merely a matter of opinion in no wise affecting the faith. For the teaching of the Doctors on the sacrament of the altar is inculcated very forcibly by the Church in its liturgy, and the very act of the eucharistic sacrifice itself, by its rites as well as by its formulae, corroborates this teaching with the whole weight of its sovereign authority.

"The Christian sacrifice is one throughout the world; for the Christian by whom it is offered is one, and there is one God to whom it is offered, one faith by which it is offered, and one alone who is offered, wrote Peter the Venerable. It is the "sacrifice of the Church", "of the whole Church", of pastor and people, of the present, of the absent. And its purpose again is unity, for it is for the Church once more that it is offered, for a greater, more united Church: *pro totius mundi salute*. "Inexpressible mystery of divine grace that effects salvation", says a preface in the Ambrosian liturgy. "The offerings of many become by the infusion of the Holy Spirit the one Body of Christ, and that is why we who receive the Communion of this holy bread and chalice are knit into one sole body."

The ceremonies of the Pontifical Mass at Rome were from this point of view particularly striking, as Duchesne has shown:

> It was a matter of importance in the Roman Church that the ritual of the communion should contain a clear and striking expression of ecclesiastical unity. Hence the custom of the *fermentum*, that is of sending consecrated bread from the bishop's Mass to the priests whose duty it was to celebrate in the *Tituli*; hence also the significance of the rite of the *Sancta*, that is of putting into the chalice at the *Pax Domini* a fragment consecrated at the preceding Mass and brought forth at the beginning of the present one. Thus, in all the churches of Rome, and at every assembly there for liturgical worship past or present, there was always the same Sacrifice, the same Eucharist, the same Communion. Thus, in order to show clearly that the bread broken and distributed away from the altar was the same as that which had been consecrated on the altar, a fragment of it was allowed to remain on the holy table.

For a like symbolical reason, before taking communion to the people the archdeacon poured into the large chalice reserved for this use a few drops of the consecrated wine which the Pontiff had left in his chalice for the purpose. At least that is the meaning which Duchesne attaches to this rite, which dates back to about the eighth century, though, as Andrieu is inclined to think, it is possible that originally it was done for reasons of convenience.

If these ceremonies of antiquity no longer portray for us in our daily Mass the unity of the Church in space and time, of pastor and people, itself a symbol of that mystic unity of which the sacrifice of the altar is the bond that is ever renewed, there is none the less no lack of prayers in the liturgy to remind us of the supreme effect of the Eucharist. Take that post-communion prayer of the Friday after Ash Wednesday:

> Lord, pour forth upon us the Spirit of your love, that in your mercy you may make of one mind those whom you have fed with the one bread from heaven.

Or the prayer over the offerings of Corpus Christi:

> Lord, graciously bestow upon your Church those gifts of unity and peace of which our offerings here are the symbols.

From end to end of the eucharistic prayer itself the same thought is uppermost, from the *Communicantes* of the Roman Canon and the post-consecration invocations of the second, third, and fourth eucharistic prayers down to the our Father and the kiss of peace. If the liturgists of olden days seem to display what to us nowadays is a disconcerting subtlety, it must yet be acknowledged that even when they made use of the strangest and most arbitrarily allegorical explanations they could still take their inspiration, as did their brethren the exegetes, from the analogy of faith. Thus Amalarius, followed immediately by Rhabanus Maurus, explaining the signs of the Cross made by the priest over the chalice with the consecrated host, tells us that the four sides of the chalice are one by one touched by the host to show that the body of Christ reunites the whole human race, gathered together from the four points of the compass into one same body, and so effects the peace of the Catholic Church. Many other examples could be found of such a simple variation on that same fundamental and essential theme.

These prayers of our Roman and vernacular liturgy repeat what was said in those of the ancient liturgies. Our evidence for the official prayer of the first centuries is only too scanty, but a particularly valuable fragment has recently been discovered. It is a homily of Theodore of Mopsuestia which is almost contemporary with the well-known Catecheses of St Cyril of Jerusalem. It describes the rite of the Mass in detail; in it we find that the priest, at the culminating point of the sacred action, prays earnestly for union and concord among all those who take part in the mystery of unity. Another Eastern rite, the liturgy of St Basil, at the same solemn moment says the same thing in almost identical terms: "May all of us who partake of this one bread and chalice be united to one another in the communion of the same Holy Spirit." That same desire is echoed in the epiclesis of an ancient Armenian liturgy:

> We beseech thee, O Lord, send thy Holy Spirit upon us and upon these present gifts so that, by sanctifying this bread and this chalice . . . he may make all of us who partake of this one bread and one chalice indissolubly one.

Or again in the so-called liturgy of St Eustace, in the prayer immediately before the kiss of peace:

> O God of mercy and forbearance, we cry to thee in unison: grant us that we may bestow peace upon each other in the holy kiss . . . make of us one holy people, save us by uniting us with one another, that we may sing thy praises.

In the West the anaphora of the "Apostolic Constitutions" takes us right back to the beginning of the third century. It is possible that it portrays the use of the Church of Rome towards the end of the second century. There is the same petition as in the Eastern liturgies:

> Send down thy Spirit, O Lord, on the sacrifice of this community. Gather it together, unite it, and grant to all the saints who rejoice in it that they may be filled with the Holy Spirit.

This too was the theme of the oldest eucharistic form (apart from the references in the New Testament) that has come down to us; it is to be read in chapters nine and ten of the *Didache*. But is this wonderful prayer, which approximates very closely to the Jewish forms of blessing at meals, really a eucharistic prayer? There has been a good deal of discussion on the point. In any case it is the basis of so many other prayers which are certainly eucharistic; and it is to be found, almost word for word, in the anaphora contained in the Euchologion of Serapion of Tmuis, an Egyptian bishop of the fourth century who was a friend of St Athanasius. For this reason alone it merits quotation here:

> Just as this bread was spread about over the mountains, and being gathered together became one, so may thy Church be gathered together from the ends of the world into thy kingdom. . . . Remember thy Church, O Lord, and gather it, made holy, from the four winds into thy Kingdom.

That is the desire with which the Spirit of Christ fills the hearts of those he has gathered together. And the same thing happens when it is no longer the Church offering Christ, but Christ offering his Church, when, that is, the sacrifice of the Head follows that of the members. For Christ offers his Church, as of old Jephthah offered his only daughter, whenever one of his members bears witness to him. And this is as true of the "official" martyr as it is of one whose torturers believe themselves to be the authorized defenders of God and his Christ—such cases have come to light in the lives of the saints. There can be few more moving phrases than the declaration, so full of gravity in its utter simplicity, made by a martyr of Saragossa as he gave himself up to the executioner: *In mente me habere necesse est Ecclesiam ab oriente usque in occidentem diffusam.*

That is the sacrifice for which the sacrifice of the altar is a preparation. True eucharistic piety, therefore, is no devout individualism. It is, according to St Thomas Aquinas, "unmindful of nothing that concerns the good of the Church". With one sweeping, all-embracing gesture, in one fervent intention it gathers together the whole world. It recalls the commentary that, according to St John, Jesus himself gave when he instituted the sacrament of his love: the allegory of the vine, the "new commandment", the prayer for unity and the approach of the "supreme token of love". It is on these things that true eucharistic piety bases thoughts and resolutions; it cannot conceive of the action of the breaking of bread without fraternal communion: *in communicatione fractionis panis.*

Finally, it should be noted that in the ancient liturgies, and now again in the new Eucharistic Prayers, the prayers for union form the culminating point of the Epiclesis:

> May all of us who share in the body and blood of Christ be brought together in unity by the Holy Spirit. (Eucharistic Prayer, II.)
>
> Grant that we, who are nourished by his body and blood, may be filled with his Holy Spirit, and become one body, one spirit in Christ. (Eucharistic Prayer, III.)
>
> By your Holy Spirit, gather all who share this one bread and one cup into the one body of Christ, a living sacrifice of praise. (Eucharistic Prayer, IV.)

The Epiclesis, like the whole of the sacrifice, but as a rule more explicitly, is under the sign of the Holy Spirit. This Holy Spirit, by whom Christ's carnal body was prepared, intervenes too in the confection of the Eucharist for the making of his Mystical Body. He who fell upon the sacrifice of Elijah as a devouring fire burns up the dross in humankind, the obstacle to the unifying power of the sacrament. And as the Spirit of Christ once came down upon the Apostles not to unite them together in a closed group but to light within them the fire of universal charity, so does he still whenever Christ delivers himself up once more "that the scattered children of God may be gathered together". Our churches are the "upper room" where not only is the Last Supper renewed but Pentecost also.

3. Ludwig Feuerbach, Protagonist of Atheist Humanism

"The word 'atheism' is applied to phenomena which are quite distinct from one another. . . . Believers themselves frequently bear some responsibility. For, taken as a whole, atheism, is not a spontaneous development, but stems from a variety of causes, including a critical reaction against religious beliefs, and in some places against the Christian religion in particular. . . . The Church strives to detect in the atheistic mind the hidden causes for the denial of God. Conscious of how weighty are the questions which atheism raises, and motivated by love for all men, the Church believes these questions ought to be examined seriously and more profoundly."—*Pastoral Constitution on the Church in the Modern World*, I, 1, 19 and 21.

Beneath the numerous surface-currents which carry contemporary thought in every direction, it seems possible to detect a deep undercurrent, by no means new—or rather a sort of immense *drift*; through the action of a large proportion of its foremost thinkers, the peoples of the West are denying their Christian past and turning away from God. This is not the everyday type of atheism which crops up in all ages and is of no particular significance; nor is it the purely critical atheism so fashionable in the last two hundred years: for, though the effects of this are still conspicuously in evidence today, it does not replacing a living force, since it is manifestly incapable of replacing what it destroys—its only function being to hollow out a channel for that other atheism which is my real subject. Contemporary atheism is increasingly positive, organic, constructive. Combining a mystical immanentism with a clear perception of the human trend, it has three principal aspects, which can be symbolized by three names: Auguste Comte, Ludwig Feuerbach (who must share the honour with his disciple, Karl Marx) and Friedrich Nietzsche.

The negation which underlies positivist humanism, Marxist humanism and Nietzschean humanism is not so much *a*theism, in the strict sense of the word, as *anti*theism, or, more precisely, antichristianism. Great as the contrast is between them, their common foundation in the rejection of God is matched by a certain similarity in results, the chief of which is the annihilation of the human person.

First and foremost, then, it is suggested that Christians should take cognisance of the spiritual situation of the world in which they are involved. It is recognized that Positivism is an immense edifice of scientific philosophy and practical politics; that Marxism, which has received its Summa if not its Bible in *Das Kapital*, is a vast and powerful system of political and social economy; and that Nietzsche's ideas offer an extraordinary profusion of pedagogic resources (in the profoundest sense of the term). There are many elements to be found in all three to which a Christian, as such, is not required to define his attitude; there are many others, often mutually contradictory, which he would have the right to claim as his own, after rescuing them from the synthesis which has warped them. They contain many audacities which do not frighten him. And, even at their most blasphemous, they advance criticisms whose justice he is bound to admit.

Feuerbach and Marx, like Comte and Nietzsche, were convinced that faith in God was disappearing for ever. That sun was sinking on our horizon never to rise again. Their atheism both believed and rejoiced in its own finality, having, it thought, this advantage over former atheisms, that it discarded everything, even to the problem which had brought God to birth in man's consciousness. They were antitheists like Proudhon, but in a still more radical way; and they did not come to his conclusion that the existence of God, like that of man, "is proved by the eternal antagonism between them". They did not share his sense of the militant return of mystery after each attempt to overcome it. Beneath the variety of its manifestations, their "humanism" seems equally lightless. Yet the sun did not cease to rise!

Man cannot organize the world for himself without God; without God he can only organize the world *against man*. Exclusive humanism is inhuman humanism. Moreover, it is not the purpose of faith in God to install us comfortably in our earthly life that we may go to sleep in it. On the contrary, faith disturbs us and continually upsets the too beautiful balance of our mental conceptions and our social structures. Bursting into a world that perpetually tends to close in upon itself, God brings it the possibility of a harmony which is certainly superior, but is to be attained only at the cost of a series of cleavages and struggles coextensive with time itself. "I came not to bring peace, but a sword." Christ is, first and foremost, the great disturber. That certainly does not mean that the Church lacks a social doctrine, derived from the Gospel. Still less does it tend to deter Christians, who, like their brothers, are men and members of the city, from seeking to solve the city's problems in accordance with the principles of their faith; on the contrary, it is one more necessity impelling them to do so. But they know at the same time that, the destiny of man being eternal, he is not meant to find ultimate repose here below.

1. *A Tragic Misunderstanding*

A wonderful piece of sculpture adorning the cathedral of Chartres represents Adam, head and shoulders barely roughed out, emerging from the earth from which he was made and being moulded by the hands of God. The face of the first man reproduces the features of his modeller. This parable in stone translates for the eyes the mysterious words of Genesis. "God made man in his own image and likeness."

From its earliest beginnings Christian tradition has not ceased to annotate this verse, recognizing in it our first title of nobility and the foundation of our greatness. Reason, liberty, immortality and dominion over nature are so many prerogatives of divine origin which God has imparted to his creatures. Establishing man from the outset in God's likeness, each of these prerogatives is meant to grow and unfold until the divine resemblance is brought to grow and unfold until the divine resemblance is brought to perfection. Thus they are the key to the highest of destinies.

"Man, know thyself!" Taking up, after Epictetus,

the Socratic *gnōthi seauton*, the Church transormed and deepened it, so that what had been chiefly a piece of moral advice became an exhortation to form a metaphysical judgement. Known yourself, said the Church, that is to say, know your nobility and your dignity, understand the greatness of your being and your vocation, of that vocation which constitutes your being. Learn how to see in, yourself the spirit, which is a reflection of God, made for God. In the words of St Gregory of Nyssa:

> O man, scorn not that which is admirable in you! You are a poor thing in your own eyes, but I would teach you that in reality you are a great thing! . . . Realize what you are! Consider your royal dignity! The heavens have not been made in God's image as you have, nor the moon, nor the sun, nor anything to be seen in creation. . . . Behold, of all that exists there is nothing that can contain your greatness.

Philosophers have told man that he is a "microcosm", a little world made of the same elements, given the same structure, subject to the same rhythms as the great universe; they have reminded him that he is made in its image and is subject to its laws; they have made him into part of the mechanism, or at most, into an epitome of the cosmic machine. Nor were they completely mistaken. Of man's body, it is true. But if man digs deeper, he will be amazed at the depths opening up within him. Unaccountable space extends before his gaze. In a sort of infinitude he overflows this great world on all sides, and in reality it is that world, "macrocosm", which is contained in this apparent "microcosm" . . . *in parvo magnus*. That looks like a paradox borrowed from one of our great modern idealists. Far from it. First formulated by Origen, then by St Gregory Nazianzen, it was later repeated by many others. St Thomas Aquinas was to give much the same translation of it when he said that the soul is in the world *continens magis quam contenta*—containing it rather than contained by it—and it found fresh utterance through the lips of Bossuet.

Man, to be sure, is made of dust and clay; or, as we should say nowadays, he is of animal origin—which comes to the same thing. The Church is not unmindful of this, finding a warrant for it in the same passage of Genesis. Man, to be sure, is also a sinner. The Church does not cease to remaind him of that fact. The self-esteem which she endeavours to instil into him is not the outcome of a superficial and ingenuous view of the matter. Like Christ, she knows "what there is in man". But she also knows that the lowliness of his origin in the flesh cannot detract from the sublimity of his vocation, and that, despite all the blemishes which sin may bring, that vocation is an abiding source of inalienable greatness. The Church thinks that this greatness must reveal itself even in the conditions of present-day life, as a fount of liberty and a principle of progress, the necessary retaliation upon the forces of evil. And she recognizes in the mystery of God-made-man the guarantee of our vocation and the final consecration of our greatness. Thus in her liturgy she can celebrate each day "the dignity of the human substance" even before rising to the contemplation of our rebirth.

These elementary truths of our faith seem commonplace today—though we neglect their implications all too often. It is difficult for us to imagine the disturbance they created in the soul of man in the ancient world. At the first tidings of them humanity was lifted on a wave of hope. It was stirred by vague premonitions which, at the recoil, sharpened its awareness of its state of misery. It became conscious of deliverance. To begin with, needless to say, it was not an external deliverance—not that social liberation which was to come, for instance, with the abolition of slavery. That liberation, which presupposed a large number of technical and economic conditions, was brought about slowly but surely under the influence of the Christian idea of man. "God," says Origen, in his commentary on St John, "made all men in his own image, he moulded them one by one." But from the outset that idea had produced a more profound effect. Through it, man was freed, in his own eyes, from the ontological slavery with which Fate burdened him. The stars, in their unalterable courses, did not, after all, implacably control our destinies. Man, every man, no matter who, had a direct link with the Creator, the Ruler of the stars themselves. And lo, the countless Powers—gods, spirits, demons—who pinioned human life in the net of their tyrannical wills, weighing upon the soul with all their terrors, now crumbled into dust, and the sacred principle which had gone astray in them was rediscovered unified, purified and sublimated in God the deliverer! It was no longer a small and select company which, thanks to some secret means of escape, could break the charmed circle: it was mankind as a whole which found its night suddenly illumined and took cognizance of its royal liberty. No more circle! No more blind hazard! No more *Fate*! Transcendent God, God the friend of men, revealed in Jesus, opened for all a way which nothing would ever bar again. Hence that intense feeling of gladness and of radiant newness to be found everywhere in early Christian writings. It is much to be regretted that this literature should be so remote from us today. What wealth and force our faith is forfeiting by its ignorance of, for instance, the hymns of triumph and the stirring appeals that echo in the *Protrepticus* of Clement of Alexandria!

But if we look down the course of the ages to the dawn of modern times we make a strange discovery. That same Christian idea of man which had been welcomed as a deliverance was now beginning to be felt as a yoke. And that same God in whom man had learnt to see the seal of his own greatmess began to seem to him like an antagonist, the enemy of his dignity. Through what misunderstanding and distortions, what mutilations and infidelities, what blinding pride and impatience this came about, would take too long to consider. The historical causes are numerous and complex. But the fact remains, simple and solid. No less than the Early Fathers, the great medieval scholars had exalted man by setting forth what the Church had always taught of his relation to God: "In this is man's greatness, in this is man's worth, in this he excels every creature." (Aeminas.) But the time came when man was no longer moved by it. On the contrary, he began to think that henceforward he would forfeit his self-esteem and be unable to develop in freedom unless he broke first with the Church and then with the Transcendent Being upon whom, according to Christian tradition, he was dependent. At first assuming the aspect of a reversion to paganism, this urge to cut loose increased in scope and momentum in the eighteenth and nineteenth centuries until, after many phases and many vicissitudes, it came to a head in the most daring and destructive form of modern atheism: absolute humanism, which claims to be the only genuine kind and inevitably regards a Christian humanism as absurd.

This atheist humanism is not to be confused with a hedonist and coarsely materialist atheism—a commonplace phenomenon to be found in many periods of history. It is also quite contrary in principle—if not in its results—to an atheism of despair. But it would be dangerous to call it a critical atheism and let it go at that. It does not profess to be the simple answer to a speculative problem and certainly not a purely negative solution; as if the understanding, having, on the attainment of maturity, set itself to reconsider the problem of God, had at last been obliged to see that its efforts could lead to nothing. The phenomenon which has dominated the history of the mind during the last few centuries seems both more profound and more arbitrary. It is not the intelligence alone that is involved. The problem posed was a human problem—it was *the* human problem—and the solution which is being given to it is one that claims to be positive. Man is getting rid of God in order to regain possession of the human greatness which, it seems to him, is being unwarrantably withheld by another. In God he is overthrowing an obstacle in order to gain his freedom.

Modern humanism, then, is built upon resentment and begins with a choice. It is, in Proudhon's word, an "antitheism". In Proudhon, this antitheism operated first of all in the social field, where it was chiefly a struggle against a false idea of Providence. It was a refusal to be resigned to the "economic contradictions", productive of poverty, for which a more or less conscious conspiracy on the part of economists and property-owners claimed the sanction of heaven and which they sometimes even went so far as to extol as "harmonies". Thus Proudhon laid the blame not so much upon God himself as upon a certain form of recourse to his authority. Subsequently extending his conception to the metaphysical field, he still thought that God was "inexhaustible": the struggle in which man necessarily wrestled with God was an "eternal struggle"; "the hypothesis of a God" was reborn every time "from its resolution in human reality"; always, after the denials and exclusions, there was a resurgence of something beyond man—Proudhon for the most part called it Justice—which imposed itself upon man and prevented him from ever taking himself for God.

Thus Proudhon, even when undergoing the influence and appropriating the language of those whom he calls "the humanists" or "the new atheists", expressly refuses to follow them. Antitheism, as conceived by them, is something more radical. They go further in opposition and denial because they set out from a more complete refusal. The story is a dramatic one. At its maximum point of concentration, it is the great crisis of modern times, that same crisis in which we are involved today and which takes its outward course in disorder, begets tyrannies and collective crimes, and finds its expression in blood, fire and ruin.

2. *Feuerbach and the Religious Illusion*

Let us now take a look at one of the protagonists of the drama, the nineteenth-century German thinker, Ludwig Feuerbach. Considered solely in himself, he would hardly deserve more than an honourable place, which has never been denied him, in a good history of philosophy. But his importance is chiefly due to the fact that he was the stepping-stone between the great current of speculation known as German idealism and the great current of revolutionary thought and action which were to be its principal, if not its most legitimate, heir. Feuerbach pulled down the Hegelian structure and he did not found the communist movement. Between Hegel and Marx he is rather shadowy figure—even if, as Engels wrote in his study of him, he was, of all the immediate descendants of Hegel, "the only one who amounted to anything as a philosopher". For all that, he is the link connecting Marx with Hegel, and the "transformer", thanks to whom Hegel finds his continuation in Marx, though with a change of direction.

In the years that followed Hegel's death in 1831, the focus of philosophical debates was the problem of God, and it was on this subject, and not primarily on political or social matters, that the split occurred between the right and left wings of Hegelianism. Feuerbach soon assumed the leadership of the left. His purpose ran parallel to that of his friend Friedrich David Strauss, historian of the origins of Christianity. As Strauss tried to account historically for the Christian illusion, Feuerbach tried to account psychologically for the religious illusion in general. or, as he himself put it, to find in anthropology the secret of theology. The substance of what Strauss said, in his *Life of Jesus* (1835), was that the gospels are myths expressing the aspirations of the Jewish people. In *Religion* Feuerbach was to make the parallel assertion that God is only a myth in which the aspirations of the human consciousness are expressed. "Those who have no desires have no gods either. . . . Gods are men's wishes in corporeal form."

To explain the mechanism of this theogony, Feuerbach had recourse to the Hegelian concept of "alienation". But, whereas Hegel applied it to absolute Spirit, Feuerbach, reversing the relation of the idea to the real, applied it in *The Essence of Christianity* to man in his flesh and blood. Alienation, according to him, is for man the fact of finding himself "dispossessed of something essentially belonging to him for the benefit of an illusive reality" (Daniélou). Wisdom, will, justice and love, says Feuerbach, are so many infinite attributes which constitute man's own being and which nevertheless affect him "as if it were another being". Thus he spontaneously projects them beyond himself and objectifies them in a fantastic form, the pure product of his imagination, to which he gives the name of God. In this way he defrauds his own self. "It is one and the same act which strips the world of its content and transfers that content to God. The poor man possesses a rich God" or, to be more accurate, he impoverishes himself by enriching his God, in filling whom he empties himself. He "affirms in God what he denies in himself". "Religion is thus transformed into a vampire which feeds upon the substance of mankind, its flesh and its blood" (Spenlé).

Such action on the part of man was, moreover, inevitable and therefore justified in occurring when it did. In the Hegelian rhythm it represents the second movement of the dialectic, the phase of denial or antithesis which necessarily precedes the synthesis in which man is to regain possession of his essence, now enriched. Feuerbach knew that this stage could not be skipped. Thus he does not execrate religion in the past but recognizes in it "an essential aspect of the human spirit". Without religion, without the worship of an external God, man would never have had more than a dim and muffled consciousness like that of an animal, for, "strictly speaking, consciousness exists only in beings which can make their essence and their species the object of their thought". It was first necessary to realize one's duality, as it were—which amounts to losing oneself in order to find oneself. But one day the alienation must come to an end. After the movement of religious systole, by which man rejected himself, he must now, by a movement of diastole, "take back into his heart that nature which he had rejected". The hour has at last struck when he must exorcize the phantom. Reflection carries on the work begun by a spontaneous impulse. The kingdom of man has come.

For Feuerbach, then, God is only the sum of the attributes which make up the greatness of man. The Christian God carries this to perfection (and that is why man has never been more alienated than in Christianity, the worst of religions because the highest). He is "the mirror of man", he is "the great book in which man expressed his loftiest thoughts, his purest feelings". In a maximum closely reminiscent of Auguste Comte's law of the three states,

Feuerbach wrote in *Religion*: "God was my first thought, reason my second, and man my third and last." In *The Essence of Christianity* he says, "It is the essence of man that is the supreme being. . . . If the divinity of nature is the basis of all religions, including Christianity, the divinity of man is its final aim. . . . The turning-point of history will be the moment when man becomes aware that the only God of man is man himself. *Homo homini Deus*!"

Be it noted, however, that Feuerbach does not say, as Max Stirner was soon to say, *Ego mihi deus*. He believes that the human essence, with its prerogatives which call for worship, is not inherent in the individual considered in isolation, but only in the community, in the generic being (*Gattungswesen*); indeed, by substituting for that generic being the illusion of an external God, it is the mistaken religion which is responsible for disintegrating mankind into a dust of individuals, thus leaving each of them to himself and turning him into a being naturally isolated and thrown back upon himself; for "man spontaneously conceives his own essence as individual in himself and generic in God; as limited in himself and infinite in God". But when, abandoning that chimerical view, man comes actually to participate in the common essence, to that extent he really assumes divinity. Thus the principle which sums up real religion is a principle of practical action: it is a law of love, which takes the individual out of himself and obliges him to find himself in fellowship with those of his own species. It is the principle of an altruist morality. For, in the last analysis, "the distinction between human and divine is neither more nor less than the distinction between the individual and makind". Thus Feuerbach clears himself of the charge of preaching egoism.

He is equally on the defensive against the charge of preaching atheism. Insofar as the term is a negative one, he rejects the title of atheist. In his view this name should rather be applied to the idolater, who mistakenly regards himself as a true believer. Such a man, without faith in the divinity of qualities, feels the need to attach them to an imaginary subject, which he takes as the object of his worship:

> The true atheist is not the man who denies God, the subject; it is the man for whom the attributes of divinity, such as love, wisdom and justice, are nothing. And denial of the subject is by no means necessarily denial of the attributes. The attributes have an independent significance of their own; by their value they force men to recognize them; they impose themselves upon him; they immediately convince his understanding that they are true in themselves; they are their own warrant, their own guarantee. . . . A quality is not divine because God possesses it; God must possess it because without it he would be an imperfect being. . . . When God, as subject, is the thing determined, and the attribute is the determinant, it is not to the subject but to the attribute that the rank of supreme being, of divinity, really belongs.

The inference is that, in order not to sacrifice love to "God", we must sacrifice "God" to love. In so doing, moreover, we shall be accomplishing the secret purpose of religion. For, rightly understood, religion "ceremoniously unveils the hidden treasures of man's nature; it is the avowal of his inmost thoughts, it is the public revelation of the secrets, the mysteries of his love".

Thus, far from being unfaithful to the spirit of Christianity, which is the perfect religion, we shall at last explain its mystery.

Feuerbach had at first intended to give a different title to *The Essence of Christianity*, the first of the works in which he expressed his essential idea. It was to be called *Gnōthi seauton*—a truly symbolic point. His atheistic humanism thus took as its banner the old precept which the Fathers of the Church had taken over, long before. To reveal to mankind its own essence in order to give it faith in itself—that was his sole aim. But in order to attain it he thought it necessary to overthrow the God of the Christian conscience. Towards the end of his life he wrote: "The only thing I am anxious to leave in the memory of man after my death is my fundamental thought. I will let everything else go. . . . All that I want is to have introduced one single idea into the speech of conscious humanity." It must be recognized that he succeeded only too well.

He had an immediate following. Engels mentions the extraordinary "impression of deliverance" felt by many young men of his generation in November

1841, on reading *The Essence of Christianity*. Hegel's disciples were at that time laboriously threshing about in the toils of contradiction. "At one blow it was demolished." This was a potent stimulus. "There was widespread enthusiasm," Engels adds. "We all straightway became Feuerbachians." He is scarcely exaggerating. The impression made on people was of something final; of a perfectly clear revelation, as if the scales had at last fallen from all eyes; of a full stop put to discussions that had been going on for a thousand years and had suddenly become pointless; of an end to the illusion of religious faith and the adventures of idealist speculation. The solution to the human problem had been found; there was nothing left to look for.

What had happened in Germany very soon happened in Russia also. We learn from Dostoevsky's *Journal of an Author* that Bielinsky, until then the uncontested master of the younger generation, revered Feuerbach and Strauss. Later, Herzen was to recount how Feuerbach, read at Novgorod, was responsible for his innermost transformation, so that he turned "from mysticism to the most ruthless realism". From 1843 we find Bakunin, then a refugee in Switzerland, explaining that communism is only Feuerbach's humanism carried into the social field; he extolled Feuerbach for having made the great pronouncement on religion that Hegel had failed to arrive at, and for having thereby put an end to "the mirage of God", thus giving back to the earth what heaven had stolen from it. Bakunin adopted Feuerbach's doctrine in its entirety and forty years later he was still trying to popularize it. Comparing Feuerbach with Auguste Comte, he marvelled at the agreement between these "two great minds", though "they had never heard of each other"; and in his tract on *Dieu et l'Etat* he wrote:

> The heaven of religion is nothing but a mirage in which man, uplifted by ignorance and faith, rediscovers his own image, but magnified and transposed—in other words, deified. . . . Christinanity is the religion of religions because, in its fullness, it lays bare and reveals the nature, the peculiar essence, of every religious system; that is to say, the impoverishment, the enslavement and the annihilation of mankind for the benefit of the deity. . . . God appears, man is extinguished, and the greater the godhead, the more wretched man becomes. That is the history of all religions; that is the effect of all divine inspiration and divine lawgiving. In history the name of God is the terrible club with which men of manifold inspiration, the great genuises, have struck down the liberty, dignity, reason and prosperity of men. . . .

From the outset, too, Karl Grun had become a missionary of the same doctrine in Paris, where he lived as a refugee. As Ruge had sought to convince Louis Blanc, so he tried to convince Pierre Leroux. It was no good; but, in the fever of his zeal, he fancied that, to make up for it, he had achieved a more important conversion, namely that of Proudhon—

which was true only to a very limited extent. (Almost immediately after their conversation Proudhon set about refuting Feuerbach, whose importance he did not deny, but whose philosophy had hardly more effect upon him that Strauss's exegesis. From its first page *The Philosophy of Poverty* adopts a standpoint very definitely opposed to Feuerbach's humanism.) In England Engels was an active propagandist; he championed the cause of his master in atheism with Carlyle while George Eliot translated *The Essence of Christianity*. Among those of a later generation, Chernichevsky, the chief forerunner of Russian communism, went through the same school and recognized in Feuerbach the first of his great Western masters. But the disciple who eclipsed all others was Karl Marx.

In *The Holy Family*, written in collaboration with his friend Engels and published in 1845, Marx warmly praises his master for having dispelled "the old quibbles" and set up man in their place. Feuerbach, to be sure, never went deeply into economic problems. While clearly indicating the social import of his doctrine, he left it to others to make it explicit. To the young men who brought him their reforming impatience and wanted him to join them in the fight, he replied in the Introduction to his collected works in 1846: "The only ills I cure are those that come from the head or from the heart; it is from the stomach that men suffer chiefly, I know, and anything that does not help to eradicate that fundamental ill is mere useless rubbish. Must my complete works be considered as among such rubbish, then? I'm afraid so. But are there not many ailments, even of the stomach, which come from the head? I have set out, once for all, to attack the maladies of humanity's head and heart. But what you have set out to do you should carry out conscientiously, keeping faith with yourself." Thus Feuerbach cannot be regarded as the founder of Marxism in all but name. But its "spiritual father" he certainly is.

It is true that Marx very soon broke with his friends, the "young Hegelians", who contented themselves with daring speculations and political radicalism; it is true that he broke with his own past and bade the philosophy of his youth and all speculation a farewell which was at the same time a declaration of war, and that he even, to some extent, renounced his first works, including, maybe, the articles Feuerbach had inspired. But for all that he did not go back upon the conclusions he owed to *The Essence of Christianity*. They always remained for him something final. Not that he did not criticize Feuerbach's doctrine: but when he did so it was not to call it in question in the slightest degree; it was only to pronounce it incomplete and still too abstract and vague. He reproached it with making religious alienation in some sort a metaphysical act, instead of explaining it more positively as a sociological fact. He endeavoured to go beyond what Engels irreverently called Feuerbach's "banalities" by substituting, as Otto Ruhle said, the "materialism of social situations" for the "materialism of the objective data of nature". To quote Engels' book on Feuerbach once more, Marx wanted to replace "the cult of abstract man", which was the centre of Feuerbach's new religion, "by the science of real men and their historical development". Thus he stripped from the human essence the mystic halo with which Feuerbach had kept it surrounded. Soon everything else seemed to pale, in his thought, before the technique of economics and the tactics of class warfare. No other philosophical or religious influence, however, made any profound change in the thesis of humanist metaphysics which he had taken over from his master. If he hardly ever referred to it again after reaching his maturity, this was because it seemed to him a thing settled once for all, a starting-point at which there was no further need to linger. Thus it remains true that "Marx traces his spiritual descent from the humanist religion of Feuerbach" (Vignaux). He cannot be accounted for in any other way. And that spiritual fact is fraught with the gravest consequences; it is among those which dominate the history of our times.

Nor did Marx content himself with admiring what he called the "inspired demonstration" by which the mystification of men's minds was at last brought to an end, or with extolling Feuerbach as a second Luther in the history of human emancipation. He stated that Feuerbach went "as far as a theorist can go without ceasing to be a theorist and philosopher", and that after him "the criticism of religion is substantially complete"; in 1844 he took Feuerbach's work under his protection, in *The Holy Family*, where he instituted a complete defence of it against Bruno Bauer, improving upon the dithyrambic eulogy he had already bestowed upon it two years earlier, in his short anonymous article on "Luther as umpire between Strauss and Feuerbach". He not only copied his master's religious criticism in his own social criticism, analysing the "secular form" of alienation to arrive at the conclusion that humanity must abolish the State as it had abolished religion; he adapted the Feuerbachian conception of religion to social life.

For him, too, as he states in his *Critique* of Hegel's philosophy, "man makes religion, it is not religion that makes man; religion is in reality man's own consciousness and feeling which has not yet found itself or has lost itself again". Such is "the foundation of religious criticism". Only:

> Man is not an abstract being outside the real world. Man is the world of men, the State, society. This State and this society produce religion, a mistaken attitude to the world, because they themselves constitute a false world. Religion is the general theory of this world, its encyclopaedic compendium, its popular logic, its spiritual point of honour, its inspiration, its moral sanction, its solemn completion, its general consoling and justifying reason. . . . It is the imaginative realization of the human essence, because that essence has no true reality. The misery of religion is, on

> the one hand, the expression of real misery and, on the other, a protest against real misery. Religion is the sigh of the creature overwhelmed by unhappiness, the soul of a world that has no heart, as it is the mind of an era that has no mind. It is the opium of the people.

Thus, at the rebound, the fight which must be put up against religion will be a "fight against this world", against "this perverted world whose spiritual aroma is religion". "Atheism is humanism mediatized to itself through the suppression of religion"—a thoroughly Feuerbachian way of putting it. But, in order that man may one day be freed from the mystical illusion and all the evils it brings with it, Marx thinks it is necessary to transform society, since it is bad social organization which is the true cause of human belief and consequently of human alienation. Or, rather, its two forms, social alienation and spiritual alienation, help to produce each other and it is impossible to overcome one without attacking the other. And this results in a combined struggle, the two parts of which serve each other as means to an end. "The only point on which I do not agree with Feuerbach," Marx wrote to Ruge on 13 March 1843, "is that, to my mind, he attaches too much importance to nature and not enough to politics." And again in *The German Ideology* he says that Feuerbach "does not see that the perceptible world surrounding him is not a direct datum, from all eternity and always the same, but is the product of industry and of the state of society, and is so in the sense that, in every period of history, it is the result and product of the activity of a whole succession of generations, each of which lifted itself on the shoulders of the one before, whose social order it changed in accordance with changing needs. . . . He never arrives at active man, really existing, but always stops short at an abstract idea. . . . He offers no criticism of the conditions of actual existence. . . ."

Thus, in preaching practical means of emancipating man, Marx may be said to have shown himself "more Feuerbachian than Feuerbach himself". In that way he ensured his own success in revolutionary circles and, right to the end, he remained faithful to his inspiration, thanks to the addition which he thus made to it in point of method. Marx's doctrine, never plain naturalism, always paid as much attention to man's spiritual life as to his material existence. His communism offered itself as the only concrete realization of humanism; it quite deliberately claimed to be a total solution for the whole human problem; moving to the plane of reality, it did not propose to figure there only as a social phenomenon but as a spiritual phenomenon also. This is what gives it greatness but this is also the radical flaw in it; it is this that bathes even its sound elements in a baneful atmosphere and it is this that chiefly arouses Christian opposition. "The religion of the workers has no God", Marx wrote in a letter to Hardmann, "because it seeks to restore the divinity of man."

The combination of French socialism, English economics and German metaphysics might have produced something quite different from Marxism, if Marx had not found a master in Feuerbach. It was through Feuerbach that his feet were firmly planted on one of the slopes of the Hegelian system. It has been said that, before being the right-wing Hegelian who sees in dogmas the symbols of his philosophy, Hegel had been for a short time the left-wing Hegelian who wants to destroy dogmas in order to make way for truth. In one of his earliest writings, noting man's need, first of all, to think his way "out of his own consciousness", he made this short but lucid observation which seems to forecast the double programme of Feuerbach and Marx: "It was one of the merits of our age that, at least in theory, it claimed as man's property the treasures that had been squandered on the heavens; but what age will have the strength to take practical advantage of that right and secure that property?"

The second part of the prophecy presupposed the realization of the first. Feuerbach was indispensable to Marx. Arnold Ruge's play on the name—*Feuerbach* means "stream of fire" or "burning brook"—was repeated by Karl Grün and by Marx himself, and offers the historian a suggestive symbol: on the threshold of the Marxist paradise there is the purgatory of Feuerbach.

4. The Family of God

"The people fully incorporated into the society of the Church are those who, possessing the Spirit of Christ, accept its entire system and all the means of salvation which have been granted to it, and through union with its visible structure are joined to Christ, who rules it through the Supreme Pontiff and the bishops."—*Dogmatic Constitution on the Church*, II, 14.

The story is told of a priest who, shortly after apostatizing, said to a visitor who was about to congratulate him: "From now onward I am no more than a philosopher—in other words, a man alone." It must have been a bitter reflection, but it was true. He had left the home outside which there will never be anything save exile and solitude. Many people aren't aware of it, because they live in the passing moment, alienated from themselves, rooted in this world like seaweed on the rocks. The preoccupations of daily life absorb them; the golden mist of appearances forms a veil of illusion around them. Sometimes they look in a hundred and one different places for some substitute for the Church, as if to deceive their own longings.

Yet the man who hears in the depths of his being the call which has stimulated his thirst for communion—indeed, the man who does no more than sense it—grasps that neither friendship nor love, let alone any of the social groupings that underlie his own life, can satisfy it. No more can the arts, or philosophizing, or independent spiritual exploration;

for these are only symbols, the promise of something other than themselves, and into the bargain, deceptive symbols whose promise is not fulfilled. Such bonds as these are either too abstract or too particularized, too superficial or too ephemeral; they are all the more powerless in proportion as they have the greater pull. There is nothing created by man and nothing on man's level which can wrench him free from his solitude; it grows deeper the more he discovers concerning himself.

God did not make us to remain within the limits of nature, or for the fulfilling of a solitary destiny; on the contrary, he made us to be brought together into the heart of the life of the Trinity. Christ offered himself in sacrifice so that we might be one in that unity of the divine Persons. That is to be the recapitulation, regeneration and consummation of all things, and outside that anything which exerts a pull over us is a thing of deception.

And there is a place where this gathering together of all things in the Trinity begins in this world; "a family of God" (Eph 2:19; etc.), a mysterious extension of the Trinity in time, which not only prepares us for this life of union and gives us a sure guarantee of it, but also makes us participate in it already. The Church is the only completely "open" society, the only one which measures up to our deepest longings, and in which we can finally find our whole shape. The people united by the unity of the Father and the Son and the Holy Ghost: that is the Church. In Origen's words, it is "full of the

Trinity". The Father is in the Church as the Principle to whom it is united, the Son as the medium in which it is united, the Holy Spirit as the knot by which all things are united; and all is one.

It is not only that we *know* this; we already have an anticipatory *experience* of it in the obscurity of faith. For us, according to the mode which suits our earthly condition, the Church is the very realization of that communion which is so much sought for. It guarantees not only our community of destiny but also our community of vocation; the bonds with which it seems to bind us have no other aim than freeing us, uniting us and giving us room to breathe. It is the matrix which forms that unity of the Spirit which is no more than a mirage if there is not unity of the body as well. It is the "perfect dove", like the Holy Spirit himself; in its unity we all become one, as the Father and Son are one. Hence the fullness conveyed by the joyful words in which we bind ourselves to the gift which we receive from heaven—"Amen to God". When we have entered the holy dwelling, whose dimensions are vaster than those of the universe, and have become members of the Mystical Body—

> . . . we have at our disposal for loving, understanding and serving God not only our own powers but everything from the blessed Virgin in the summit of heaven down to the poor African leper who, bell in hand, whispers the responses of the Mass through a mouth half eaten away. The

whole of creation, visible and invisible, all history, all the past, the present and the future, all the treasure of the saints, multiplied by grace—all that is at our disposal as an extension of ourselves, a mighty instrument. All the saints and the angels belong to us. We can use the intelligence of St Thomas, the right arm of St Michael, the hearts of St Joan of Arc and St Catherine of Siena, and all the hidden resources which have only to be touched to be set in action. Everything of the good, the great and the beautiful from one end of the earth to the other—everything which *begets* sanctity (as a doctor says of a patient that he has *got* a fever)—it is as if all that were our work. The heroism of the missionary, the inspiration of the Doctors of the Church, the generosity of the martyrs, the genius of the artists, the burning prayer of the Poor Clares and Carmelites—it is as if all that were ourselves; it is ourselves. All that is one with us, from the North to the South, from the Alpha to the Omega, from the Orient to the Occident; we clothe ourselves in it, we set it in motion. All that is in the orchestral activity by which we are at one and the same time revealed and made as nothing. In the core of the vast gathering of Christianity there is to be found the equivalent of all that which, in the individual body, is entrusted to the choir of cells—nourishment, respiration, circulation, elimination, appetite. The Church transposes, and paints outside us on a vast scale, all that is in us almost without our knowing it. Our brief and blind impulses are weeded, taken up again, interpreted, developed, by vast stellar movements. Outside ourselves we can decipher at astronomic distances the text written on a microscopic scale in the further depths of the heart. *Paul Claudel Interroge le Cantique des Cantiques.*

Beyond all realization at the human level and in spite of the tearing-apart which is the wages of sin and the way of redemption, the mystery of communion is in action. In its very visibility the Church is the vital nucleus around which gather from age to age, and in ways often hidden from us, all those who are to be saved. Those whom it has already united are truly the soul of the world, the soul of this great human body; as the second-century author of the *Epistle to Diognetus* put it: "Christians are in the world what the soul is in the body. The soul is spread into all the members of the body as Christians are spread in the cities of the world. . . . Christians are as if held in the prison of the world; yet nonetheless it is they who bear up the world. . . . The post God has assigned to them is so noble that they are not allowed to desert it."

There is an amazing boldness in such an assertion; the Christian who made it was the voice of a tiny flock, wretched and persecuted, and considered beneath contempt by the wise and the powerful of the world. It is true that this small group was growing rapidly; it gathered fresh members every day and a shrewd observer might have foreseen even then that before long it would swamp the Empire. But this was not the foresight which gave to the writer of the Epistle his sure and serene audacity. There was no question of any prophetic insight into any earthly future; it was purely a matter of faith, and an awareness of speaking in the name of the Church of God. We may say that he spoke as an "ecclesiastic" in the true sense.

As far as our current speech is concerned, that term is much worn, not to say debased. It has become a professional title for entry in official registers, the appropriate label that goes with a particular dress. Even within the Church we scarcely ever use it save as a purely external descriptive term. One wonders who will give it back its breadth and dignity, and make us aware once more of the associations which it once called to mind. In the original sense of the term, the "ecclesiastic"—the *vir ecclesiasticus*—is a churchman, without any obligatory distinction into layman or cleric. He is a man in the Church; better, a man of the Church, a man of the Christian community. If this sense of the word cannot be altogether salvaged from the past, the reality signified should at any rate remain. It is much to be hoped that a sense of it will revive among us.

"For myself," said Origen, "I desire to be truly ecclesiastic." He thought—and rightly—that there was no other way of being a Christian in the full sense. And anyone who is possessed by a similar desire will not find it enough to be loyal and obedient, to perform exactly everything demanded by his profession of the Catholic faith. Such a man will have fallen in love with the beauty of the House of God; the Church will have stolen his heart. It is his spiritual native country, his "mother and his brethren", and nothing that concerns it will leave him indifferent or detached; he will root himself in its soil, form himself in its likeness and make himself one with its experience. He will feel himself rich with its wealth; he will be aware that through the Church and through the Church alone he participates in the unshakeableness of God. It will be from the Church that he learns how to live and die. Far from passing judgement on it, he will allow it to judge him, and he will agree gladly to all the sacrifices demanded by its unity.

a. Our Catholic Ancestry

Being a man of the Church, he will love the Church's past. He will meditate over its history, holding its tradition in reverence and exploring deep into it. Granted, the last thing he will do will be to devote himself to a cult of nostalgia, either in order to escape into an antiquity which he can reshape as he likes, or in order to condemn the Church of his own day, as if it were already grown decrepit and its Bridegroom had cast it off. Any attitude of that kind will repel him, spontaneously. He may, certainly, take pleasure in going back in spirit to the age of the newborn Church when, as St Irenaeus put it, the echo of the Apostles' preaching was still audible, and "Christ's blood was still warm and faith burned with a living flame in the heart of the believer."

But for all that he will be sceptical about those myths of the Golden Age which give such a stimulus to the natural inclination to exaggeration, righteous indignation and facile anathematizing. In any case, he knows that Christ is always present, today as yesterday,and right up to the consummation of the world, to continue his life, not to start it again; so that he will not be forever repeating, "It was not so in the beginning." His questionings are not directed to a "dumb Church and dead Doctors", and he will have no "petrifaction" of Tradition, which is for him no more a thing of the past than of the present, but rather a great living and permanent force which cannot be divided into bits. He will of course never take it into his head to appeal from the present teaching of the magisterium to some past situation, doctrinal or institutional, or invoke such things in order to apply to that teaching an interpretation which would in fact be an evasion; for he will always accept the teaching of the magisterium as the absolute norm. For he believes both that God has revealed to us in his Son all that is to be revealed, once and for all, and that, nonetheless, divine thought, in the words of Jean Levie, S.J. "adapts the understanding of the mystery of Christ at each epoch, in the Church and through the Church". Thus he will grasp firmly the fact that although the Church does not, in the exercise of its magisterium, propose to us anything newly invened, so also "the Church says nothing on its own account"and does not claim to be itself "the true source of revelation", as it is sometimes wrongly said to do, and blamed for doing, It only follows and declares the divine revelation "through the interior direction of the Holy Ghost who is given it as its Teacher" and "those who are afraid that it may abuse her power in order to establish falsehood, have no faith in Him by whom she is ruled" (Bossuet).

He will view Scripture, Tradition and the Magisterium as the one and only threefold channel by which the World of God reaches him; and he will see that, far from damaging one another or imposing limitations on one another, these three things provide mutual support, establishing order among themselves, confirming, elucidating and exalting. He will see that their fates are bound up together, and will recognize in them the threefold cord which cannot be broken. But he will not consider that his total loyalty to the magisterium lets him out of making and keeping a contact at depth with the Church's tradition, any more than it excuses him from the study of the Scriptures, which will always be the soul of real theology. The magisterium itself constantly encourages him to maintain such a contact, and in it he is looking for something other and something more than the results of scientific investigation.

He knows that ecclesiastical culture in the true sense is never come by without a loving and disinterested knowledge of what may rightly be called the "classics" of his faith. What he will look for is not so much the company of great intellects as that of truly spiritual men, and so he will, as far as possible, get on to intimate terms with those who prayed to Christ and lived, worked, thought and suffered for Christ in the Church before him; for such men are the fathers of his soul. By often keeping their company he will acquire something at least of that Catholic ethos, lack of which neither knowledge of the scientific type nor orthodoxy itself can compensate for. Any man who does this will really understand, for example, the enthusiasm of Newman when, in his Anglican days, he discovered the true Church in "the Church of the Fathers" and, through a sort of Platonic reminiscence (or rather an illumination from the Holy Spirit), recognized in it his spiritual mother.

Whether we like it or no, there are many nonessential things which change according to time and place. But without blinding himself to the plain fact of this diversity, the man of the Church will make it his business to see also the continuity which exists at an even deeper level of reality. There will, of course, be no question of excluding from view anything the Church approves of, while on the other hand he will also have his personal preferences, being aware of affinities which God has doubtless not willed in vain, and cultivating such. But for all that he will always give special attention to certain facts and periods of particular importance; the age of the first martyrs, the rise of monasticism, the main stages in the formation of dogma, the work of the great saints and Doctors, the big spiritual revivals, and so on. He will take into account the history of missionary expansion, in its main outlines at least, and he will not forget the ancient tradition of eastern Christianity, the basic stratum, the massive main trunk from which we all spring. If he is himself a scholar, he will put to the best use he can the method of his own particular discipline, though he will never lose sight of the fact that Catholic tradition does not open the whole of its secret even to an exhaustive enquiry, and that it becomes fully intelligible only to him who keeps in the line of its axis and studies it from the inside as one who lives by the faith of the Church.

b. Catholic Solidarity

Since he is a man of the Church he will not acquire a culture of this type just for interest's sake, taking pleasure in it, as St Clement of Alexandria says, "as one who tours the monuments of a great city". On the contrary, he will be wholly at the service of the great community, sharing its happiness and its trials, and taking part in its battles. He will always be on guard against allowing the upper hand, in himself, or about him, if he can help it, to a sensibility more alive to the causes of this world than the cause of Christ. He will cultivate in himself and try to encourage in his fellows the sense of Catholic solidarity; with a particular horror of anything that looks like esotericism. He will resist the pull of the world, and a sure instinct will lead him to recognize spiritual danger in good time.

He will not be a fanatic, of course, and he will have no time for mere showing-off; still, he will be aware that in the sacraments of the Church he has received not a spirit of fear but one of power, and in consequence he will have no hesitation in joining battle for the defence and the honour of his faith. Since he knows that it is possible to sin much by omission, he will speak and act boldly "in season and out of season", even at the risk of displeasing many people —even at the risk of being misunderstood by those whose agreement he values most highly. He will, of course, carefully avoid all situations whose danger has been pointed out for him by competent authority. But he will also bear in mind the positive duties of which that authority reminds him—duties whose urgency he can see for himself, but which he might be inclined to neglect in the light of a purely human prudence. *He will always want to be ready to give any man a reason for the hope that is in him*, as St Peter urged in the early days, and will be wary of making himself unable to do so by getting used to too narrow a world, or by concern for his own peace.

He will always make it his concern to think not only "with the Church" but "in the Church", as St Ignatius put it—which implies a deeper faith, a closer participation and, *ipso facto*, a more spontaneous behaviour—that of a real son, of someone who is at home. He will always let himself be enlightened, guided and shaped, not by habit or convention, but by dogmatic truth; he may be as much aware as the next man, even more than the next man, of the "difficulties of religion"—as was Newman; but he will be no more capable than Newman of making a real connection between "apprehending those difficulties, however keenly . . . and on the other hand doubting the doctrines to which they are attached". He will be no more tempted than Newman was "to break in pieces the great legacy of thought thus committed to us for these latter days" by men like St Ireneaus, St Athanasius, St Augustine and St Thomas; rather, he will make it his business to preserve it and draw attention to it. He will be anxious to show those who cling to it with a care that is sometimes a cowardice, that this inheritance is even richer and more fruitful than they think. On the other hand, he will reject all modern self-sufficiency and any kind of doctrinal liberalism.

c. Catholic Breadth

But in a true man of the Church the uncompromisingness of the faith and attachment to Tradition will not turn into hardness, contempt or lack of feeling. They will not destroy his friendliness, nor will they shut him up in a stronghold of purely negative attitudes. He will take care to remember that in its members the Church should be nothing but a "yes", as it was in its Head, all refusal being nothing more than the other side of a positive affirmation. He will not give way to the spirit of compromise any more than the Church does, but like it he will always want to "leave open every door through which minds of different kinds may reach the same truth" (Gilson).

He will not want to "disquiet . . . them who are converted", any more than it does, and this much-to-be-desired moderation, identical with that of the Apostle James at the Council of Jerusalem, will seem to him not only more human and wiser, but also more respectful of the plan of God than can be the demands of a certain type of zealous Catholic.

Following its example, he will refuse to develop a craze over one single idea, like a common-or-garden fanatic, since like the Church, he believes that there is no salvation save in balance, as is indeed shown by the whole of dogma and confirmed by the whole history of heresy. He will be equally careful not to confuse orthodoxy or doctrinal firmness with narrow-mindedness or intellectual apathy, echoing the words of St Augustine: "A thing is not right just because it is hard," and he will remember that one of his duties is to "elucidate for the men of his time the things necessary for salvation", as St Ignatius put it.

He will take great care that some generalized idea does not gradually come to take the place of the Person of Christ; careful though he is concerning doctrinal purity and theological precision, he will be equally careful not to let the mystery of faith be degraded into an ideology; his total and unconditional faith will not come down to the level of a sort of ecclesial nationalism. And when he pauses for self-examination he will be very much on the look-out against the fatal mistake of those "theologians" who having become "wise and prudent . . . make the Gospel a scientific objective and flatter themselves to have a knowledge of it possessed of a greater perfection than that of the mass of the faithful", while all the time "it is often they themselves who have the least understanding of it in the sense which Christ had in mind" (Grou).

He will hold himself apart from all coteries and all intrigue, maintaining a firm resistance against those passionate reactions from which theological circles are not always free, and his vigilance will not be a mere mania of suspicion. He will understand that the Catholic spirit, which is at the same time both rigorous and comprehensive, is a spirit which is charitable rather than quarrelsome, in distinction from every kind of spirit of faction or mere sectarianism, whether the aim of it be to evade the authority of the Church or, on the contrary, to make a corner in it.

For a man of this kind all praiseworthy initiative, every new enterprise that is duly approved, and every new centre of spiritual vitality, is an occasion for giving thanks. He will be no friend of the "itch for . . . controversy" because he will be well aware that the devil (who has a whole art of sowing disorder) shows brilliant skill in disturbing the body of the Church under cover of speculative debate; he will dread the false rigorism that hides the unity at depth which exists in spite of it, and will not show himself hostile on principle to legitimate diversity. He will, on the contrary, consider it necessary—"provided", as St Anselm says, "that the unity of charity in the Catholic faith be preserved"—for we cannot wipe out "the diversity of human sensibility"; he will even regard it as beneficial, "so that the manifold wisdom of God may be made known through the Church" (Eph 3:10). He will not transform these diversities—by means of a narrow and superficial logic—into oppositions and contradictions, but see them, rather, as finding completion and fusion in the "bond of love": "Those who are like Christ are alike among themselves with a magnificent diversity" (Claudel). If he were to take it upon himself to reduce everything to uniformity, he would consider himself as marring the beauty of Christ's Bride.

Even when it so happens that these diversities do become divergences, he will not start to worry as soon as the Church starts to feel them. He will not have to reflect for very long to see that they have always existed in the Church and always will; and that if they were ever to come to an end it would only be because its spiritual and intellectual life had come to an end. Far from losing patience, he will try to keep the peace, and for his own part make a big effort to do that hard thing—retain a mind bigger than its own ideas. He will cultivate "that sort of freedom through which we transcend what involves us most remorselessly" and which is "a mysterious, winged, ironic way of transcending our differences" (Maritain).

And if he is not to despair of managing this even where are concerned minds seriously divided, he will—all the more so—be confident of doing it where his brothers in the faith are concerned. By that very fact he will be protected against the terrible self-sufficiency which might lead him to see himself as the incarnate norm of orthodoxy, for he will put the indissoluble bond of Catholic peace above all things and will hold it a black mark against himself to tear the seamless robe even by the smallest "schism of charity".

Even when controversy cannot be avoided he will see that it does not embitter him, and that the actions of those whom St Paul already described as "false brethren" will not provide him with an excuse for using weapons like theirs. For he will always remember that "the wisdom that is from above, first indeed is chaste, then peaceable, modest, easy to be persuaded", that charity is "without disimulation" and that "the fruit of justice is sown in peace". His whole behaviour will show that the spirit of power which he has received is also "a spirit . . . of love and of sobriety". If only from experience, he will know well that there is no trusting in men, but the depressing proofs of this will not dim his joy as the years accumulate them; for God himself is the Maintainer of that joy, and the devotion he has sworn to the Church cannot but be purified by this particular experience.

Since he is a member of a body, he will be responsive to what affects the other members, whatever his own place and function may be. Anything that bears hard upon the body as a whole, or paralyses it, or damages it, affects him too, and he can no more be indifferent to it than be can be amused by it.

Thus he suffers from the evils inside the Church, and he will want the Church, in all its members, to be ever purer and more closely united, more attentive to the demands of the soul, more active in witness, more passionate in the thirst for justice; in all things more spiritual and further yet from all concession to the world and its falseness. He will want to see it always celebrating a pasch of "sincerity and truth" in all its members.

For him there will be, of course, no question of cherishing utopian dreams, and *he will always direct his accusations against himself first and foremost*; yet he will not resign himself to Christ's disciples' settling down in the all-too-human, or stagnating outside the great currents of humanity. He will see the good, be glad of it, and set himself to making it visible to others, but without blinding himself to the faults and sufferings which some try to deny while others are scandalized by them; he will not consider that loyalty or simply experience of human nature obliges him to condone every abuse. And he will, moreover, be aware that the mere passing of time wears out many things, so that many innovations are necessary if dangerous novelty is to be avoided, and that a reforming impulse is natural to the Church. Since he is not obsessed with the past, he will have no desire for change—or any experiment with a view to it—in those things that are of time; rather, he will make an effort at the discernment of spirits, searching with those who search. He will be wary of possible opposition to the work of God through a severity which is too quick off the mark or too unbending, and take care not to bring to a halt some necessary advance because it has been marked by a false step or two; his instinct will always be to redirect an impulse rather than repress it.

But for all that, he will not evade his duty if circumstances call on him to intervene. He will only take care that he is not moved by some impulse other than that of faith. He will be aware—sometimes agonizingly aware—of the twofold nature of his responsibility. He will dread equally either impoverishing in souls the Christian faith by which they should live, or making that faith intolerable to them by demands which are unjustified. Yet the very thing which gives rise to this kind of perplexity is also the thing that carries him through it.

A man of the Church will always remain open to hope; for him, the horizon is never closed. Like St Paul, he will want to be full of rejoicing in his sufferings, and will go so far as to believe himself called, in this manner—as all are called—to "fill up those things that are wanting in the sufferings of Christ . . . for his body, which is the Church". knowing that in Christ he has "the hope of glory" (Col 1:24, 27). In common with the community of believers, he waits for the return of him whom he loves, and he does not lose sight of the fact that everything should, in the last analysis, be judged with reference to that end. But at the same time he is aware that this waiting is an active waiting and should not divert us from any of the things to be done in this world. On the contrary, it makes those things more urgent and demanding. It certainly does not imply (as some people appear to think) neglect of the duties of the present, lack of interest in this existence or a putting of charity into cold storage until the end of the world.

He will welcome and make his own, at depth, the pre-occupation with truth, authenticity and "poverty of spirit" which are characteristic of an age "in which", as P. R. Régamey, O.P., says, "the great fear of a well-formed soul is of imposture, and this more in the sphere of the sacred than in any other". As one who has had a way opened to the Heavenly Jerusalem, the "city of truth" where he had encountered the "God of truth", "the true God in whom there is no lie", he will bear in mind that the Holy Spirit is the enemy of all deceit (Wis 1:5), and that Christ Himself put good faith along with justice and mercy (Mt 23:23) as constituting together the three most important precepts; and he will shun the pious fraud in all its forms—though he will also understand the value of silence.

He will realize that there is a moment for everything; that the best of undertakings can be wrongly timed, and that when the Church checks him it is not for him to pass judgement in the matter. Thus he will not be bewildered if he sometimes has to "sow in tears". Even when what he does receives the utmost approval he will want to remember always that just as he reaps what has been sown by others before him, so he must not count on gathering in even where he has sown. And last, he will hold out against the temptation offered by the over-simplified solution which in some way compromises the fullness, balance, and depth of the Catholic heritage, even when it does not touch the faith directly.

d. Catholic Obedience

The man of the Church does not stop short at mere obedience; he loves obedience in itself, and will never be satisfied with obeying, as à Kempis says, "of necessity and without love". For the fact is that all action which deserves the description "Christian" necessarily unfolds itself over a basis of passivity. The Spirit from whom it derives is a Spirit received from God. It is God himself, giving himself to us in the first place so that we may give ourselves to him; insofar as we welcome him into ourselves we are already not our own.

This law is verified in the order of faith more than anywhere else. The truth which God pours into our minds is not just any truth, made to our humble human measure; the life which he gives us to drink is not a natural life which would find in us the wherewithal to maintain itself. This living truth and this true life only find foothold in us by dispossessing us of ourselves; if we are to live in them we must die to ourselves, and that dispossession and death are not only the initial conditions of our salvation; they are a permanent aspect of our life as renewed in God.

And this essential condition is brought about, *par*

excellence, by the effect of Catholic obedience. In that obedience there is nothing of this world and nothing servile; it submits our thoughts and desires, not to the caprices of men, but to "the obedience of Christ". Fénelon says justly: "It is Catholicism alone which teaches, fundamentally, this evangelical poverty; it is within the bosom of the Church that we learn to die to ourselves in order to live in dependence." An apprenticeship of this sort never comes to an end; it is hard on nature, and those very men who think themselves most enlightened are the ones who have most need of it (which is why it is particularly healthy for them), so that they may be stripped of their false wealth, "to humble their spirits under a visible authority".

This is perhaps the most secret point in the mystery of faith, and that which is hardest of access to a mind which has not been converted by the Spirit of God. So that it is scarcely surprising that many men consider the exercise of authority in the Church as an intolerable tyranny. Moreover, whether the unbeliever condemns it or admires it, he cannot but form a very misleading idea of it, for, as Yves de Montcheuil has observed, "if the Church were only a human society, even though the most venerable and experienced ever known", its demands would not be justified. For his part, the Catholic knows that the Church commands only because it obeys God. He wants to be a free man, but he is wary of being one of those men who make liberty "a cloak for malice". He knows, too, that obedience is the price of freedom, just as it is the condition of unity: "He who is not bound by this chain," says St Augustine, "is a slave." He will be careful to distinguish it from its counterfeits and caricatures—unfortunately all too freely current—and his aim will be to please not men but God.

History and his own experience combine to show him both the desire for the knowledge of divine things which stirs the human spirit, and the weakness which lays that spirit open to falling into every kind of error. In consequence he appreciates the benefit of a divine magisterium, to which he freely submits. He thanks God for having given him that magisterium in the Church, and experiences a foretaste of the peace of eternity in placing himself under the eternal law by the obedience of faith.

He will make the appropriate evaluation of the scope of each one of the acts of the hierarchy—numerous and varied as they are—without splitting them up one from another or setting them in mutual opposition; he will accept them all as obedience demands and understand them as obedience understands them, never adapting an argumentative attitude where obedience is concerned, as if there were some question of defending at all costs a threatened autonomy. He will not countenance any contest with those who represent God, any more than he would with God himself.

Even in the grimmest cases—in such cases most of all, in fact—he will find a certain harmony of what seems to be imposed from outside and what is inspired from within; for the Spirit of God does not abandon him, any more than the Spirit of God ever abandons the Church as a whole, and what he does in the Church as a whole is also what he does in each Christian soul. The baptismal instinct of the child responds with a leaping joy to the demands made upon it by its Mother: "Wherever the Spirit of the Lord is, there also is freedom."

Even when doctrine is in no sense involved—in the day-to-day sphere of exterior activity where the question is one of decisions whose object is in itself a matter for discussion—the man who has the real spirit of obedience will not spend any longer than he can help over considerations at the human level which, however shrewd and sensible, cannot in the long run fail to obscure the light of faith.

Even though he can neither obscure them nor always hold all of them as of no account—a supernaturalized attitude is not something built up on the ruins of commonsense—he will, for all that, rise above the contingencies which are in danger of coming between him and pure divine will. He will have confidence in his superiors and make it his business to see their point of view from the inside. Whether or no there be a bond of natural sympathy between him and them, he will owe them a sincere affection and try to make less onerous for them a responsibility from which his own soul benefits; bearing in mind the axion "to perceive the person is to remove the burden of obedience", he will see in them Christ himself.

Granted, the aid given to the Church by the Holy Spirit is no guarantee that he will never have any orders to carry out save those arising from the wisest possible choices—the history of the Church is not that kind of idyll, and there would be something rather absurd about it if it were. Yet it does not matter whether the man who gives him a command in the name of God be right or wrong, obtuse or clearsighted, pure or mixed in his motives, determined (in his heart of hearts) to act justly, or not—as long as that man is invested with legitimate authority and does not command him to do evil, it is certain that it will be wrong to disobey.

And the man of the Church knows that, as Pope St Gregory the Great says, though obedience "can never oblige us to do anything evil" it can "cause us to interrupt or omit the good which we were doing or wanted to do". That is something which he knows in advance, and with a conviction of faith which nothing can shake; and history confirms the fact with a whole series of examples both good and bad. Even if this truth is in certain cases a hard one, it is, as far as he is concerned, first and foremost a wonderful truth. Certainly, as long as the order is not final he will not abandon the responsibilities with which he has been invested by his office or circumstances. He will, if it should be necessary, do all that he can to enlighten authority; that is something which is not merely a right but also a duty, the discharge of which will sometimes oblige him to heroism. But the last word does not rest with him. The Church, which is his home, is, in Origen's words, a "house of obedience".

If then he find himself prevented from realizing some apparent good, he will remember that even if his action be justified, it is not that action which matters. The work of redemption, to collaboration in which he has been called by God, is not subject to the same laws as human undertakings. And ultimately all he has to do is to take his place in the divine plan by which God leads him, through his representatives; thus, he cannot fail to have a share in "the infallible security of Providence". In the last analysis no man can ever betray a cause, or break faith with another man, himself, or God, when he simply obeys. There will be no sophism, no appearance of good or persuasion of justification which can cut off from the man of the Church the light of St Paul's words when he proposes for our imitation Christ made obedient.

He can never forget that the salvation of mankind was accomplished by an act of total self-abandonment, and that the author of that salvation, "whereas he was indeed the Son of God . . . learned obedience by the things which he suffered" (Heb 5:8), and that it is through him alone, with him alone and in him alone that we can be "at one and the same time the saved and those who save" (*Mystici Corporis*). The mere recalling of this fact carries more weight with him than any amount of theory and discussion; it will always be a safeguard against his reducing Christian obedience—which is conformity with the obedient Christ—to a virtue which is primarily of social importance.

For to see nothing more in it than that particular aspect—which is, of course, most certainly there—will be, in his eyes, a misunderstanding of its most valuable element.

A true son of the Church will not, of course, be preoccupied to excess with these extreme cases (which must nonetheless be taken into account if the principle of Catholic obedience is to be understood in its pure state). Even where he has a duty to act, and in consequence a duty to judge, he will on principle maintain a certain distrust with regard to his own judgement; he will take good care to have himself in hand, and if it so happens that he incurs disapproval he will, far from becoming obstinate, if necessary accept the fact that he cannot clearly grasp the reasons for it. He will apply to himself on such occasions this homely truth —that even with the best of intentions we can still grossly deceive ourselves (or perhaps simply fail to take everything into account), and that it is a healthy thing to be warned of the fact. And finally he will under all circumstances be much aware that he cannot be an active member of this Body if he is not, first and foremost, a submissive member, quick and easy in response to the direction of the head. Even if he is submissive to all that is obligatory, he will not be content to carry on his work in the odd corners of his community, as it were. He will not grant himself the right to call himself a son of the Church unless he is, first of all and always, a child of the Church, and that in all sincerity.

Here we come upon the fundamental distinction

that the Church is a community, but in ordereb to that community it is first a hierarchy. The Church which we call our Mother is not some ideal and unreal Church but this hierarchical Church itself; not the Church as we might dream it but the Church as it exists in fact, here and now. Thus the obedience which we pledge it in the persons of those who rule it cannot be anything else but a filial obedience. It has not brought us to birth only so as to abandon us and let us take our chance on our own; rather, it guards us and keeps us together in a maternal heart. We continually live by it spirit, in Bérulle's words, as "children in the womb of their mothers live on the substance of their mothers". And every true. Catholic will have a feeling of tender piety towards it. He will love to call it "mother"—the title that sprang from the hearts of its first children as the texts of Christian antiquity bear witness on so many occasions. He will say with St Cyprian and St Augustine: "He who has not the Church for mother cannot have God for Father."

When a Catholic wants to expound the claims which the Church has on his obedience, he feels a certain embarrassment, or rather a certain melancholy. It is not that its title-deeds are inadequate. But when taken in the dryness of the mere letter the claims don't do justice to something which is, as far as he is concerned, essential. He can comment on the illuminating complex of Scripture texts, point to the facts of history, develop the arguments that are suitable to the occasion. But when he has done all this, all he has done is to establish the fact that we ought to submit, as a matter of justice and our own good; he has not been able to convey the spontaneous leap of his own heart to obedience, nor the joy which he feels in his submission. He has established an obligation, but he has not communicated an enthusiasm. He may have justified the Church, but he hasn't been able to make its true character understood from within.

If he is to do that he must achieve much more. If he is to overcome the revulsion of the "natural man", he will have to turn his argument into a channel for the living witness of his own faith; he will have to show the splendour of the Catholic vision. The Church which is the bringer of the good news and the bearer of life must not be presented as a domineering power or a pitiless drawer-up of rules. He must not be content with giving a precise explanation of how the Church's authority is in principle neither arbitrary nor extrinsic; he must go on to give some idea at least of how, through the exercising of that power, each one of the faithful is effectively sustained in his self-giving to Christ; how the fabric it weaves links each man effectively to his brethren; how all still hear today the voice of their Lord through the human voice which teaches and commands. And finally he must explain—or rather communicate some sense of—the spiritual fruitfulness of sacrifice. He must display some of the great miracles of Catholic sanctity—miracles which spring up under the shadow of obedience in the seedbed of humiliation.

e. The Head of the House

The Roman Church is the object *par excellence* of accusations of tyranny; it is even sometimes—absurdly—put on a parallel with the various systems of political absolutism. And it is also the primary object of the objections of many Christians, who nevertheless recognize the necessity of a visible authority. Conversely, it is primarily of this Church that the Catholic thinks when he calls the Church his mother. In common with tradition, he considers it as "root and mother of the Catholic Church", as "the mother and mistress of all the Churches", as "mother and mistress of all the faithful of Christ". He considers its head as "the head of the episcopate" and "the father of the Christian people"; "the master of the whole household of Christ", as St Ignatius Loyola puts it. For him, the See of Rome is the "Holy See", the "Apostolic See" *par excellence*. He knows that Peter was given the charge of not only the lambs but the sheep as well; that Christ himself prayed that the faith of Peter might not fail, and that he gave Peter the keys of the Kingdom of Heaven and the command to confirm his brethren. He realizes that Peter personifies the whole Church, and that just as each bishop is the bridegroom of his own particular Church, so Peter, the Bishop of Rome, may be said to be the bridegroom of the Universal Church, the whole of which has in him its visible foundation.

As against a frequently lodged objection (based on a misunderstanding), he will, of course, be equally clear that this visible foundation in no way prejudices that unique Foundation which is Christ, any more than the visible chief shepherd puts into eclipse the Good Shepherd, since here there is no question of duplication, the very name "Peter" having been chosen by Christ to express this identity of submission, which is in itself the fruit of faith. Believing as he does that the Church has received the promise of perpetuity and victory over death, and holding that it was the Church which was in Christ's mind in that scene on the road to Caesarea, he will naturally grasp the consequence that as long as the Church goes on building itself up and subsisting in her visible state—that is to say, as long as this world lasts—it cannot be without a visible foundation for her building. Peter was not given his office simply in order to reliquish it almost at once; he was given it to hand on after him. "In his successors—the bishops of the See of Rome, which was founded by him consecrated by his blood—he lives, presides and judges perpetually (Mansi, IV, 1296).

Finally the Catholic will not be content merely to grant and grasp that in the last analysis the Church is, so to speak, concentrated whole in Peter; the seeing of the fact will be an occasion of joy to him. He will not be worried by those who try to persuade him that he has "lost the sense of the totality of the Church", and that in submitting himself to the power of the Pope he has resigned himself to a belief which is, as it were, merely belief at the word of command—as if "in Romanism properly understood" the whole doctrine and life of the Church resided only in the single person of its head. For we do not deny the existence of a circle when we know that it must have a centre; and it is no abolishment of the body when we say that it has a head.

In short, the Catholic recognizes Peter as him who has charge of the Universal Church. That is why he holds that he is—to quote the expression given authoritative status by the First Vatican Council—"the supreme judge of the faithful", who holds the fullness of power in the Church; that is why he makes his own the words of St Ambrose: "Where Peter is, there the Church is." He will always see in Peter both the unshakeable rock upon which his own firmness is based, and the centre of Catholic truth and unity, the one and only visible centre of all the children of God. In the authority of Peter he sees the support of his faith and the guarantee of his communion. And thus his fieldity to the Christian faith finds concrete expression in his love for Peter, to whom he is bound, despite all exterior vicissitudes, by every fibre of his soul.

That picture of the Catholic in whom the consciousness of churchmanship is lively is, of course, altogether too meagre and abstract an affair, besides being—obviously—over-idealized. Here, as in all things, there is normally a big gap between the sincerest faith and the most loving disposition, on the one hand, and effective practice, on the other; for man is always an inconsequential creature. But the important thing to take note of is not the tribute we all pay, more or less heavily, to human weakness, but rather the nature and scope of our desires. The mystery of the Church and the good things it brings are always beyond what we manage to live into reality of them. We never draw upon more than a meagre part of the wealth which our Mother has at her disposal. Yet every Catholic who is not an ingrate will have in his heart that hymn of gratitude which has been given words by a great contemporary poet: "Praised for ever be that majestic Mother at whose knees I have learned all!" (Claudel).

It is she who daily teaches us the law of Christ, giving us Gospel and helping us to understand its meaning. It is hard to imagine where the Gospel would have got to or what state it would have reached us in if, *per impossibile*, it had not been composed, preserved and commented on within the great Catholic community—hard to picture the deformation and mutilation it would have suffered both as to text and as to interpretation. . . .

But there is, after all, no need to have recourse to these hypotheses; history speaks forcefully enough. There is no counting the number of aberrations which have been based upon an appeal to the Gospel, or the number of those who have, in consequence of them, toppled over into "atheistic and impious doctrines, or stupid and ridiculous beliefs". Origen had already noticed this, and that great biblical thinker did not hesitate to point a warning finger at "the temptation hidden in the reading of the sacred books", when they are not read *in the Church*. And our own day adds its own lessons to those of the past.

The meaning of the written mystery can belong only to the social unity which carried within itself the revelation of that mystery; and although we may say, with St Francis de Sales, that "Scripture is entirely adequate to teach us all things" in a certain sense, we should also add, as he did, that "it is in us that there lies the inadequacy since, without Tradition and the magisterium of the Church, we should not be able to determine the meaning which it ought to have". Thus, when we consult Tradition and listen to the magisterium it is, as Fénelon says, "not that we prefer the Church to the Scriptures, but rather the explanation of the Scriptures given by the whole Church to our own explanation".

We believe that the Word of God is "addressed to the Church", and that is precisely why we listen to it and read it *in the Church*. The Church has neither glossed over the paradoxes of the Gospel nor changed its vividness nor sentimentalized its power nor betrayed its spirit. The Church is always the paradise in the midst of which the Gospel wells up like a spring and spreads out into four rivers to make the whole earth fruitful. Thanks to the Church, the Gospel is proposed to all, both the great and the small of the world, from generation to generation, and if it does not produce in us its fruit of life, the fault is ours.

We owe our praise therefore, to this great Mother of ours for the divine mystery which she communicates to us through the twofold and ever-open door of her doctrine and her liturgy; for the centres of religious life which she brings into being, protects and maintains; for the interior universe which she discovers to us, and in the exploration of which she gives us her hand as guide; for the desire and the hope which she sustains in us, and for her purifying of our worship by unmasking and dispersing the illusions which deceive us.

She pours into us and sustains a faith which is always whole and which neither human decadence nor spiritual lassitude can touch, however deep they may go. She continually presents us with new brothers; she cares equally for all, little and great alike—the ignorant and the wise, the common-or-garden parishioner and the picked body of consecrated souls. She makes sure for us the inheritance of the ages and brings forth for us from her treasure things new and old. In her patience, she is always making a fresh start, untiringly, in her slow work of education, and gathering together again, one by one, the threads of unity which her children are always tearing apart. She protects us against the enemy who prowls around us seeking his prey; and does not hold us back for herself, but urges us on to the encounter with God, who is all love. Whatever shadows the Adversary casts, she cannot but recognize for her own the children whom she has borne, and she will have the power to rejoice in their love while they in their turn will find security in her arms. She sets in the hearts of her best children a zeal which carries them all over the world as the messengers of Christ; steers us clear of sectarian excesses and the deceptive enthusiasm which is always followed by revulsion; teaches us to love all that is good, all that is true, all that is just, and to reject nothing that has not been tested.

She re-lives from age to age the passion of her Bridegroom; exhorts us to fight and bear witness to Christ; does not hesitate to make us pass through death—from the first death, which is Baptism, onwards—in order to bear us into a higher life. For all these benefits we owe her our praise; but we owe it to her above all for those deaths which she brings us—the deaths which man himself is incapable of, and without which he would be condemned to stay himself indefinitely, going round and round in the miserable circle of his own finitude.

The Church is the Mother of love at its most lovely, of healthy fear, of divine knowledge and holy hope. Without it our thought is diffuse and hazy; but the Church gathers it together into a firm unity. It scatters the darkness in which men either slumber, or despair or—pitifully—"shape as they please their fantasies of the infinite", as Renan put it. Without discouraging us from any task it protects us from the deceptive myths of the Churches made by the hand of man, and spares us from the aberrations and the revulsions that follow them. It saves us from destruction in the presence of God; it is the living ark, the gate of the east. It is the unflawed mirror of the activity of the Most High; as the beloved of the Lord of the Universe it is initiated into his secrets and teaches us whatever pleases him.

Its supernatural splendour never fades, even in the darkest hours, and it is thanks to the Church that our darkness is bathed in light; through it, the priest goes up every day to the altar of the God who gives joy to our youth. Each day it gives us him who is the Way and the Truth, and it is through the Church that we have hope of life in him. The Church is the holy Mother, the unique Mother, the immaculate Mother, the great Mother, the holy Church, the true Eve, sole true Mother of all the living.